D0881330

Saint Basil on the Value of Greek Literature

CRANACH
The choice of Herakles (cf. p. 54)
(present location unknown)

Saint Basil
on the Value of
Greek Literature

edited by
N. G. WILSON

DUCKWORTH

First published in 1975 by
Gerald Duckworth & Co. Ltd.
The Old Piano Factory,
43 Gloucester Crescent, London NW1

© 1975 N. G. Wilson

Cloth I S B N o 7156 0872 X
Paper I S B N o 7156 0924 6

Printed in Great Britain
by W & J Mackay Limited, Chatham

Contents

Introduction

1. St. Basil (*c.* 330–379), bishop of Caesarea in Cappadocia, was one of the three Cappadocian church fathers of the fourth century who are the outstanding figures of Greek patristic writing, the others being his brother Gregory of Nyssa and his friend Gregory of Nazianzus. Among his voluminous writings perhaps the most significant is the set of rules for the monastic life which came to be generally accepted in the Greek church. Another which is certainly not unimportant is the essay edited in the following pages. Apart from the influence that it appears to have exercised on educational practice and theory over many centuries it allows us to form an idea of the opinions held by a leading figure about the crucial question in the cultural history of late antiquity, the relation of Christian and classical culture. That issue is far too complex to be discussed in the introduction of an edition planned on the scale of the present volume, and I will content myself with referring the reader to three good recent books, which, though they do not seem to me to be quite correct in their judgment about B., are not likely to be substantially misleading in their general picture (W. Jaeger, *Early Christianity and Greek paideia*, Harvard 1961 = Oxford paperback 1969; H.-I. Marrou, *Histoire de l'éducation dans l'antiquité*, ed. 6, Paris 1965, 451–71; P. Lemerle, *Le premier humanisme byzantin*, Paris 1971, 43ff.).

2. This essay is an address by B. to his nephews (and perhaps nieces). From the text itself we can gather very little about them, and there does not seem to be any other source of information. We do not know whether they were the children of more than one of B.'s nine brothers and sisters. By implication they were all much of the same age, since B. does not distinguish between them when he makes assumptions about their knowledge or powers of understanding. He presumes that they have read and will remember Hesiod

(1.14), a text that was probably read at a relatively early stage in the school curriculum. They are also expected to be capable of identifying the sophist from Ceos as Prodikos (v.55, assuming that the reading of the majority of manuscripts is sound), and, more surprising, to know that 'the Egyptian sophist' is a possible way of referring to the mythological figure Proteus (ix.141). This argues a considerable degree of knowledge, if not downright precocity. On the other hand they are said to be too young to understand a disquisition on the topic of life after death (ii.15–16). A tantalising hint occurs at v.61, where they are said to be of much the same age as Herakles was in the allegory of Prodikos, and the age implied fairly clearly in B.'s immediate source of the story, Xenophon, is somewhere in the region of fifteen or sixteen. If that hint can be pressed, it gives the answer to one of our questions.

But only one. Did B. really write for his nephews only? It is likely enough that he had his eye on eventual publication, or that he at least allowed friends, to whom he had mentioned the matter, to consult his text and take copies of it for their personal use. That was the form that publication often took in antiquity, as was inevitable before the age of printing. An author might revise his text after a time and allow a bookseller or another friend to make copies of it. In the present essay there is no sign that B. made revisions except for a phrase of dubious interpretation in 1.24, which at first sight looks like the words of a person addressing a general audience, but on further investigation proves to be far from conclusive evidence. But whatever the history of the text in B.'s own lifetime, it soon came to be part of the corpus of works regularly transmitted under his name, and it was regarded as one of his homilies. The misapprehension was not corrected until the Italian Renaissance, when the humanist Leonardo Bruni translated the work into Latin in order to make it available to a wider audience and indicated in an accompanying letter that it was originally addressed to the author's nephews.

3.   The exact title is uncertain. Most of the manuscripts call it a homily, but one calls it a paraenesis, a piece of advice. Titles in manuscripts do not necessarily have authority. The

contents suggest that it really belongs at least in part to the class of literature called protreptic, the encouragement to the philosophical or virtuous life. The manuscripts also indicate that the contents are concerned with the means of deriving benefit from Greek, that is to say pagan, literature. Some sections of the text are evidently concerned with this theme, but it is not discussed as fully as one might hope, and some modern scholars, not entirely without justification, have complained of the weakness of the argument. This weakness can hardly be denied, but it can perhaps be partly explained as the result of an attempt to combine two themes within too short a space.

4.   The date of the work is not known. The only clue to be seen in the text is B.'s statement (1.3–7) that he is now of a certain age and has been through many vicissitudes, so that he is now qualified to give advice to the young. I find it difficult to avoid the conclusion that this remark is to be attributed to the last years of a man who died at the age of about forty-eight, in other words to the middle or late seventies of the century. Otherwise it seems intolerably sententious. We may also bear in mind the consideration that, were the essay a product of the sixties, it might be rather different in tone as a result of the emperor Julian's attempts in 361–2 to interfere with the educational system.

5.   The chief propositions of the essay are as follows. In reading pagan literature one must select what is useful and avoid the rest (1.27–8 and IV.50–1). The idea that all pagan writings are harmful and to be avoided, a view taken by other fathers of the church at various dates, is not discussed, and perhaps we should infer that B. did not even think it worthy of mention. The notion of an education based entirely on Christian texts, which is the only possible explanation of the attempt by pseudo-Apollinaris to replace Homer in the school curriculum by a versified paraphrase of the Psalms and Plato by a rewriting of the Gospels in dialogue form (Socrates, *Ecclesiastical History* 3.16), is another idea which B. does not even contemplate. These omissions may be as much due to the tender age of his nephews, which made detailed

9

discussions of theory inappropriate, as to a failure by B. to consider various theories. It may be worth noting in passing that B. does nothing to encourage bowdlerisation or censorship of the kind practised by the Jesuits in their editions of the classics in the seventeenth and eighteenth centuries.

B. then defines further his notion of the utility of pagan literature by saying (II.37–9) that all types of author, whether poets, orators or other prose writers, are to be exploited if they can lead to benefit for the character. While his nephews are too young to appreciate fully the meaning of the scriptures they should study the culture of a not entirely dissimilar civilisation (II.26–30). Biblical precedents for the study of a foreign culture, Moses and Daniel, are then adduced (III). The next chapters deal with the use to be made of pagan authors; the discussion centres on the poets, but there are also anecdotes about famous pagans which are designed to point a moral and derive from a variety of prose sources. Emphasis is given to the allegory of Herakles at the fork in the road, faced by the choice between virtue and vice, which B. knew from Xenophon. B. states quite explicitly the close agreement between pagan and Christian morality at some points (VII.31–2) and that study of the former is to be regarded as suitable preliminary training for those who are to go on to appreciate the latter (VII.38–40). Despite the suggestion that some parts of pagan literature are to be avoided, the general tone of the essay does not suggest that B. is reluctantly accepting the place of the pagan authors in the school curriculum and making the best of a bad situation. At the beginning of the final chapter B. repeats his view, and if we may trust the nuance of the particles that he uses he is surprisingly modest in his attitude (X.1–4). It is true that elsewhere in his writings B. does not always seem to be of exactly the same opinion. In letter 223, written to Eustathios of Sebaste in 375, he confesses to having spent most of his youth in vain pursuits (*mataioponia*), by which he must be referring to the traditional rhetorical education, but I agree with the note of Y. Courtonne in the Budé edition of the letters, who believes that the statement cannot be taken literally and is to be regarded as an argument *ad hominem*. If so, we have here an example of what theologians term the 'economy' of B.

The relation between pagan and Christian culture in late antiquity can be illustrated by two other facts of which B. gives no hint and which are not often mentioned in modern discussions. A letter of Gregory of Nyssa (no. 15 in Pasquali's edition, cited by P. Maas in *Byzantinische Zeitschrift* 26.1926.380), addressed to two pupils of the famous pagan professor Libanios, under whom B. himself appears to have studied, reveals a fascinating literary relationship. Gregory says that he is sending a copy of his controversial writings against the heretic Eunomios in the hope that they will present it to their master and request his opinion as to its stylistic merits. This is an excellent indication of the value that the educated Christian put on the linguistic skills of the best pagan schools. The quality of B.'s own style is a pointer in the same direction. It is true that a good style was sometimes regarded as nothing more than a means of impressing the pagans. That attitude is specifically attested about a century after B.'s day in the life of Severus by Zacharias Scholasticus (*Patrologia orientalis* 2, Paris 1907, p. 46): Zacharias postponed his legal studies for a year in order to complete his literary education because it was necessary to demonstrate to pagans that Christians could achieve an equally high standard of competence in the field that the pagans might regard as their own preserve. But both B. and Gregory are anxious to achieve an Attic style in works that were not directed to a pagan audience.

6.   Plato is clearly one of B.'s main sources; the numerous verbal borrowings prove that beyond doubt. We may assume that B. was directly acquainted with the Platonic text, and did not read it in anthologies; the surviving Greek papyri do not reveal the existence of selected excerpts of Plato, nor in the present state of our knowledge is there any reason to believe that B. used forerunners of philosophical anthologies such as those made by Stobaeus. (As Max Pohlenz said in *Berliner philologische Wochenschrift* 29.1909 column 1591 'klar ist jedenfalls, dass die Kappadokier durchaus auf Plato selber

zurückgingen'.) On the other hand he may well have used an anthology as his source of anecdotes about famous individuals. It is also obvious that B. had at least a nodding acquaintance with later schools of thought such as Stoicism and Cynicism, but there is no need to search at every point for analogies between the present essay and Stoic or Cynic texts. B. will have been familiar with their ideas from his general reading. This no doubt included Plutarch as well, with whom B. shares a liking for arguments based on analogy and similes. But although Plutarch had written essays on 'The education of children' and 'Reading the poets' (*Moralia* 1–14 and 14–37 respectively), I have not found enough verbatim similarities to prove with the same degree of certainty that B. was borrowing directly from Plutarch. This, however, might be explained by supposing that B. had read one of his sources more recently than the other. (I am not therefore in substantial disagreement with the view of Max Pohlenz, *Berliner philologische Wochenschrift*, 31.1911 cols. 180–2.) In one place it looks as if we can detect him in the display of second hand learning culled from Clement of Alexandria (VIII.60), which is in no way surprising. He may also have known Iamblichus' *Life of Pythagoras* (VII.47ff.), at first sight somewhat unexpected. The account of Prodikos' allegory about Herakles at the crossroads seems to come directly from Xenophon.

7. Stylistically B. is a typical Atticist: he follows the tradition, which was well established by the middle of the second century A.D. and is seen at its best in the writings of Lucian, of imitating in vocabulary and syntax the great writers of the fifth and fourth centuries B.C. Few if any church fathers were completely immune from this fashion, which dominated Greek literature for centuries. B.'s success in writing an archaising imitation of the literary language used seven hundred years before his own time is fair. His style was good enough to deceive the Italian poet Giacomo Leopardi, one of the best Greek scholars of his day, when in 1823 he came across the text in a manuscript which lacked the title. In his vocabulary B. does employ some words that do not appear to have been used by Athenian authors of the classical

period, and he uses others in senses which they had only acquired subsequently. His syntax is not perfect: he does not understand fully the uses of the optative, and in places he seems inclined to use prepositional phrases where a simple adjective would be clear and correct. The author who influenced his style most was Plato, obviously because of his debt to Platonic ideas, but one can also detect him borrowing from Demosthenes and Xenophon. We must also presume that in order to achieve a reasonably high standard of linguistic accuracy he relied to some extent on the lexica and handbooks of Attic style, a class of literature exemplified by the surviving works of Pollux and Phrynichus.

Like other writers of the fourth century and later B. departed from the classical models by using rhythmical clausulae. The rule can be explained simply. In each clause, but especially in the final clause of a sentence, the last two accented syllables (and at this date accented is equivalent to stressed) should if possible be separated by an even number of unaccented syllables (P. Maas, *Greek metre*, Oxford 1962, 17 para. 23). The first writer to practise this rule seems to have been Himerios the sophist, who was a generation older than B. (Wilamowitz, *Hermes* 34.1889.216ff. = *Kleine Schriften* IV 56ff.). It has been shown that B.'s own practice corresponds closely to that of other well known writers of the same date (A. Cavallin, *Studien zu den Briefen des Heiligen Basilius*, Lund 1944; see especially the statistical table on p. 102).

8. Although it has never been studied in any detail, the influence of B.'s essay seems to have been very great. It was one of a long series of sermons and other works translated into Syriac in the fifth century and again probably in the seventh, and there is evidence of a translation into medieval Arabic. We may wonder whether the essay could have had much significance to an Oriental Christian, unless he was educated in a bilingual milieu; on the other hand it has to be remembered that a number of pagan literary texts were translated into Syriac, as if there were an attempt to convey the benefits of a Greek literary education in translation. The oldest surviving manuscript of the Greek text is dated to the year

13

899, and from the early tenth century until the end of the
Byzantine period, indeed as long as Greek manuscripts were
being copied in Renaissance Italy, it was widely read. In the
Bibliothèque Nationale at Paris alone there are at least
twenty-six copies, and if a count were made in all other
libraries of copies that can reasonably be dated earlier than
the year 1600, the total would probably be not far short of a
hundred. Most of these, at least in the Byzantine period
proper, contain a standard collection of B.'s homilies, in
which no special prominence is accorded to the present essay.
In the Renaissance period one sometimes finds the work
copied by itself or at any rate in a manuscript which does not
contain other writings of B., a clear indication that it was
being read for its own sake. Exactly what influence the essay
had in the middle ages is difficult to estimate, but we can
hardly be far wrong in assuming that it will have affected the
choice of texts to be read in schools and institutions of higher
learning in Byzantium, helping to preserve the classical
syllabus essentially unchanged for a millennium.

It has been remarked that if the work had been known in
western Europe in the middle ages it would have been useful
from time to time in countering ecclesiastical opposition to
classical studies, but it was not among the homilies of B.
selected for translation into Latin by Rufinus in the fifth
century. This need was met in the Renaissance by Leonardo
Bruni at the turn of the fourteenth and fifteenth centuries. In
a preface Bruni states the aim of his version clearly: it is to
invoke the acknowledged authority of a leading church
father against the perversity of those who reject humanistic
studies. The translation was influential in the fifteenth century. It was for instance cited at length by Aeneas Sylvius, the
future Pope Pius II, in his essay on the education of children
addressed to Ladislas king of Hungary in 1450. The version
perhaps circulated more widely than the original because the
number of those who were capable of reading the original
Greek was not very large, and the Latin itself was twice
turned into Italian. The Latin version was also printed several
times at the end of the fifteenth century. After the Renaissance

the work still had some influence on educational thinking. At the end of the seventeenth century Mabillon, the founder of the science of diplomatic, remarked in his *Traité des études monastiques* (part ii chapter 11) that it is the best statement by any of the early fathers on the question of the proper place of classical studies in a Christian education.

9. The present edition aims to do justice to B.'s essay by means of a more penetrating discussion of the contents and style than has previously been attempted. I hope that the notes will give linguistic help to the student who knows a little classical Greek and requires initiation into the language of the Atticist imitators. At the same time I have tried to illustrate the subject matter in a way that may be of interest also to the more advanced reader. Notes on matters of textual criticism are enclosed in square brackets. The only other edition currently available is that of F. Boulenger in the Budé series, originally published in 1935. Its introduction and very sparse notes leave a good deal to be desired, but it is greatly to Boulenger's credit that he attempted for the first time to collate a reasonably large number of manuscripts and thereby put the text on a sound basis. Given the number of manuscripts that survive it was perfectly in order for him to confine himself in the first instance to those in the Bibliothèque Nationale in Paris. I have collated six more from other libraries, including two of the oldest known, and the readings of these, though occasionally of interest, do not alter the picture established by Boulenger to any significant degree. In citing MSS. I have used the same sigla as Boulenger, but since he exhausted the alphabet I have not devised sigla for the MSS. collated by myself.

Without much doubt the best commentary on the essay is that of J. Bach in his school edition (Münster 1900). This was reissued in a revised, but not entirely superior, edition by A. Dirking (Münster 1932). I have been glad to avail myself of the material collected by these scholars. Bach collated two MSS. himself and relied on such reports of others as he could find in earlier editions. His commentary achieves a respectable level.

Saint Basil on the Value of Greek Literature

The only other important work devoted to the essay during the present century is a Munich dissertation of 1909 by G. Büttner, *Basilius des Grossen Mahnworte an die Jugend.* The author collected a great deal of material to illustrate B.'s argument and tried to show that it is chiefly dependent on Stoic and Cynic teachings, as expressed in the form of literature known as the diatribe, originally a kind of street-corner sermon. While there is no doubt that B. will have been familiar with the philosophical ideas of many schools, the fact remains that moralists of all types have much in common, and since the dependence of B. on Plato is so tangible, while he also probably draws on Plutarch, it is quite unnecessary to look further afield in tracing sources (cf. §6 above). (The book was reviewed in much these terms by M. Pohlenz, *Berliner philologische Wochenschrift* 31.1911 columns 180–2.)

10. I have to thank many friends and colleagues for their help in the preparation of this edition. In the discussion of individual passages Mr. B. P. Hillyard drew my attention to many parallels in Plutarch, the Revd. A. Meredith assisted me with information about B.'s thought and other writings, and Mr. M. D. Reeve illuminated a variety of difficulties with his acute learning. Prof. R. Kassel kindly obtained for me a xerox copy of the editions by Bach and Dirking, which I could not find in this country. Prof. K. Treu allowed me to collate the microfilm he had obtained of a manuscript belonging to the Academy of Sciences in Tiflis. Prof. Aubrey Diller made available to me his information about Greek uncial MSS., which showed that there is no uncial copy of this work still extant. Last but not least, Dr. S. P. Brock put me greatly in his debt by going through the two Syriac versions and indicating their contribution to the textual criticism of the essay.

The text is reproduced photographically from the Budé edition by F. Boulenger (Paris, Les Belles Lettres 1935). Misprints have been corrected and some other necessary improvements of the text have been incorporated.

ABBREVIATIONS

B.   = St. Basil.

Denniston = J. D. Denniston, *The Greek particles*, ed. 2, Oxford 1954.

KG   = R. Kühner—B. Gerth, *Ausführliche Grammatik der griechischen Sprache*, Satzlehre, ed. 4, Hannover 1955 (unchanged reprint of the third ed.).

LSJ   = H. G. Liddell—Robert Scott—H. Stuart Jones, *A Greek-English lexicon*, ed. 9, Oxford 1925–40, with Supplement of 1968.

Schmid = W. Schmid, *Der Atticismus in seinen Hauptvertretern*, Stuttgart 1887–97.

Lampe = G. W. H. Lampe, *A patristic Greek lexicon*, Oxford 1961–8.

PG   = *Patrologia graeca*, ed. J. P. Migne.

SB   = *Sitzungsberichte*.

Syr I refers to the earlier Syriac translation found in British Museum MSS. Add. 14543 and 17144.

Syr II refers to the later Syriac translation found in Cambridge University Library MS. Add. 3175.

Other sigla for manuscripts are explained in the appendix.

Note on orthography

It is not possible to establish precisely the orthography of Atticist authors, and it is doubtful whether they were consistent in minor details. In the present edition I have restored initial ξ in some occurrences of σύν and its compounds where it is found in good early manuscripts. Schmid 4.13–14 and 580 showed (though his information about the manuscripts probably left a good deal to be desired) that the forms in ξ were often but not invariably used by Atticists.

Nu ephelkystikon is added unnecessarily by some MSS. in several places, e.g. 1.21 φοιτῶσιν. This detail is not recorded further. Again B.'s practice is uncertain. Cf. E. Schwyzer, *Griechische Grammatik*, Munich 1939–53, 1.405.

For γίνομαι and γίγνομαι in 1.22 and elsewhere it is impossible to know what B.'s practice was. Cf. E. Schwyzer, ibid., 1.127.

At II.20 I have left πλεῖον, although LSJ makes it plain that classical Attic inscriptions have πλέον.

At VI.8 most MSS. have τοιοῦτον, which I have not altered to τοιοῦτο.

Text

ΠΡΟΣ ΤΟΥΣ ΝΕΟΥΣ
ΟΠΩΣ ΑΝ ΕΞ ΕΛΛΗΝΙΚΩΝ
ΩΦΕΛΟΙΝΤΟ ΛΟΓΩΝ

I Πολλά με τὰ παρακαλοῦντά ἐστι ξυμβουλεῦσαι ὑμῖν,
ὦ παῖδες, ἃ βέλτιστα εἶναι κρίνω, καὶ ἃ ξυνοίσειν ὑμῖν
ἑλομένοις πεπίστευκα. Τό τε γὰρ ἡλικίας οὕτως ἔχειν,
καὶ τὸ διὰ πολλῶν ἤδη γεγυμνάσθαι πραγμάτων, καὶ μὴν
καὶ τὸ τῆς πάντα παιδευούσης ἐπ' ἄμφω μεταβολῆς   5
ἱκανῶς μετασχεῖν, ἔμπειρόν με εἶναι τῶν ἀνθρωπίνων
πεποίηκεν, ὥστε τοῖς ἄρτι καθισταμένοις τὸν βίον ἔχειν
ὥσπερ ὁδοῦ τὴν ἀσφαλεστάτην ὑποδεικνύναι· τῇ τε παρὰ
τῆς φύσεως οἰκειότητι εὐθὺς μετὰ τοὺς γονέας ὑμῖν
τυγχάνω, ὥστε μήτ' αὐτὸς ἔλαττόν τι πατέρων εὐνοίας   10
νέμειν ὑμῖν, ὑμᾶς δὲ νομίζω, εἰ μή τι ὑμῶν διαμαρτάνω
τῆς γνώμης, μὴ ποθεῖν τοὺς τεκόντας, πρὸς ἐμὲ βλέπον-
τας. Εἰ μὲν οὖν προθύμως δέχοισθε τὰ λεγόμενα, τῆς
δευτέρας τῶν ἐπαινουμένων ἔσεσθε παρ' Ἡσιόδῳ τάξεως·
εἰ δὲ μή, ἐγὼ μὲν οὐδὲν ἂν εἴποιμι δυσχερές, αὐτοὶ δὲ   15
μέμνησθε τῶν ἐπῶν δηλονότι, ἐν οἷς ἐκεῖνός φησιν
ἄριστον μὲν εἶναι τὸν παρ' ἑαυτοῦ τὰ δέοντα ξυνορῶντα,
ἐσθλὸν δὲ κἀκεῖνον τὸν τοῖς παρ' ἑτέρων ὑποδειχθεῖσιν
ἑπόμενον, τὸν δὲ πρὸς οὐδέτερον ἐπιτήδειον ἀχρεῖον εἶναι
πρὸς ἅπαντα. Μὴ θαυμάζετε δὲ εἰ καθ' ἑκάστην ἡμέραν   20
εἰς διδασκάλου φοιτῶσι, καὶ τοῖς ἐλλογίμοις τῶν παλαιῶν
ἀνδρῶν δι' ὧν καταλελοίπασι λόγων συγγινομένοις ὑμῖν,

αὐτός τι παρ᾽ ἐμαυτοῦ λυσιτελέστερον ἐξευρηκέναι φημί.

Τοῦτο μὲν οὖν αὐτὸ καὶ ξυμβουλεύσων ἥκω, τὸ μὴ δεῖν
εἰς ἅπαξ τοῖς ἀνδράσι τούτοις, ὥσπερ πλοίου τὰ πηδάλια 25
τῆς διανοίας᾽ ὑμῶν παραδόντας, ᾗπερ ἂν ἄγωσι, ταύτῃ
ξυνέπεσθαι, ἀλλ᾽ ὅσον ἐστὶ χρήσιμον αὐτῶν δεχομένους,
εἰδέναι τί χρὴ καὶ παριδεῖν. Τίνα οὖν ἐστι ταῦτα καὶ
ὅπως διακρινοῦμεν, τοῦτο δὴ καὶ διδάξω ἔνθεν ἑλών.

II Ἡμεῖς, ὦ παῖδες, οὐδὲν εἶναι χρῆμα πανιάπιαϋι
τὸν ἀνθρώπινον βίον τοῦτον ὑπολαμβάνομεν, οὔτ᾽ ἀγαθόν
τι νομίζομεν ὅλως, οὔτ᾽ ὀνομάζομεν, ὃ τὴν συντέλειάν
ἡμῖν ἄχρι τούτου παρέχεται. Οὐκοῦν οὐ προγόνων περι-
φάνειαν, οὐκ ἰσχὺν σώματος, οὐ κάλλος, οὐ μέγεθος, οὐ 5
τὰς παρὰ πάντων ἀνθρώπων τιμάς, οὐ βασιλείαν αὐτήν,
οὐχ ὅ τι ἂν εἴποι τις τῶν ἀνθρωπίνων, μέγα, ἀλλ᾽ οὐδ᾽
εὐχῆς ἄξιον κρίνομεν, ἢ τοὺς ἔχοντας ἀποβλέπομεν, ἀλλ᾽
ἐπὶ μακρότερον πρόϊμεν ταῖς ἐλπίσι, καὶ πρὸς ἑτέρου βίου
παρασκευὴν ἅπαντα πράττομεν. Ἃ μὲν οὖν ἂν συντελῇ 10
πρὸς τοῦτον ἡμῖν, ἀγαπᾶν τε καὶ διώκειν παντὶ σθένει
χρῆναί φαμεν, τὰ δ᾽ οὐκ ἐξικνούμενα πρὸς ἐκεῖνον ὡς
οὐδενὸς ἄξια παρορᾶν. Τίς δὴ οὖν οὗτος ὁ βίος καὶ ὅπῃ
καὶ ὅπως αὐτὸν βιωσόμεθα, μακρότερον μὲν ἢ κατὰ τὴν
παροῦσαν ὁρμὴν ἐφικέσθαι, μειζόνων δὲ ἢ καθ᾽ ὑμᾶς 15
ἀκροατῶν ἀκοῦσαι. Τοσοῦτόν γε μὴν εἰπὼν ἱκανῶς ἂν
ἴσως ὑμῖν ἐνδειξαίμην ὅτι πᾶσαν ὁμοῦ τὴν ἀφ᾽ οὗ
γεγόνασιν ἄνθρωποι τῷ λόγῳ τις συλλαβὼν καὶ εἰς ἓν
ἀθροίσας εὐδαιμονίαν οὐδὲ πολλοστῷ μέρει τῶν ἀγαθῶν
ἐκείνων εὑρήσει παρισουμένην, ἀλλὰ πλεῖον τοῦ ἐν ἐκείνοις 20
ἐλαχίστου τὰ σύμπαντα τῶν τῇδε καλῶν κατὰ τὴν ἀξίαν
ἀφεστηκότα ἢ καθ᾽ ὅσον σκιὰ καὶ ὄναρ τῶν ἀληθῶν ἀπολεί-
πεται. Μᾶλλον δέ, ἵν᾽ οἰκειοτέρῳ χρήσωμαι τῷ παραδείγ-
ματι, ὅσῳ ψυχὴ τοῖς πᾶσι τιμιωτέρα σώματος, τοσούτῳ
καὶ τῶν βίων ἑκατέρων ἐστὶ τὸ διάφορον. 25

Εἰς δὴ τοῦτον ἄγουσι μὲν Ἱεροὶ Λόγοι, δι᾽ ἀπορρήτων

ἡμᾶς ἐκπαιδεύοντες. Ἕως γε μὴν ὑπὸ τῆς ἡλικίας
ἐπακούειν τοῦ βάθους τῆς διανοίας αὐτῶν οὐχ οἷόν τε,
ἐν ἑτέροις οὐ πάντη διεστηκόσιν, ὥσπερ ἐν σκιαῖς τισι
καὶ κατόπτροις, τῷ τῆς ψυχῆς ὄμματι τέως προγυμναζό- 3o
μεθα, τοὺς ἐν τοῖς τακτικοῖς τὰς μελέτας ποιουμένους
μιμούμενοι· οἵ γε, ἐν χειρονομίαις καὶ ὀρχήσεσι τὴν
ἐμπειρίαν κτησάμενοι, ἐπὶ τῶν ἀγώνων τοῦ ἐκ τῆς παιδείας
ἀπολαύουσι κέρδους. Καὶ ἡμῖν δὴ οὖν ἀγῶνα προκεῖσθαι
πάντων ἀγώνων μέγιστον νομίζειν χρεών, ὑπὲρ οὗ πάντα 35
ποιητέον ἡμῖν καὶ πονητέον εἰς δύναμιν ἐπὶ τὴν τούτου
παρασκευήν, καὶ ποιηταῖς καὶ λογοποιοῖς καὶ ῥήτορσι καὶ
πᾶσιν ἀνθρώποις ὁμιλητέον ὅθεν ἂν μέλλῃ πρὸς τὴν τῆς
ψυχῆς ἐπιμέλειαν ὠφέλειά τις ἔσεσθαι. Ὥσπερ οὖν οἱ
δευσοποιοί, παρασκευάσαντες πρότερον θεραπείαις τισὶν 4o
ὅ τι ποτ᾿ ἂν ᾖ τὸ δεξόμενον τὴν βαφήν, οὕτω τὸ ἄνθος
ἐπάγουσιν, ἄν τε ἁλουργόν, ἄν τέ τι ἕτερον ᾖ· τὸν αὐτὸν
δὴ καὶ ἡμεῖς τρόπον, εἰ μέλλει ἀνέκπλυτος ἡμῖν ἡ τοῦ
καλοῦ παραμένειν δόξα, τοῖς ἔξω δὴ τούτοις προτελεσθέντες, τηνικαῦτα τῶν ἱερῶν καὶ ἀπορρήτων ἐπακουσόμεθα 45
παιδευμάτων· καὶ οἷον ἐν ὕδατι τὸν ἥλιον ὁρᾶν ἐθισθέντες
οὕτως αὐτῷ προσβαλοῦμεν τῷ φωτὶ τὰς ὄψεις.

III   Εἰ μὲν οὖν ἔστι τις οἰκειότης πρὸς ἀλλήλους τοῖς
λόγοις, προὔργου ἂν ἡμῖν αὐτῶν ἡ γνῶσις γένοιτο· εἰ δὲ
μή, ἀλλὰ τό γε παράλληλα θέντας καταμαθεῖν τὸ διάφορον
οὐ μικρὸν εἰς βεβαίωσιν τοῦ βελτίονος. Τίνι μέντοι καὶ
παρεικάσας τῶν παιδεύσεων ἑκατέραν, τῆς εἰκόνος ἂν 5
τύχοις; Ἦπου καθάπερ φυτοῦ οἰκεία μὲν ἀρετὴ τῷ
καρπῷ βρύειν ὡραίῳ, φέρει δέ τινα κόσμον καὶ φύλλα τοῖς
κλάδοις περισειόμενα· οὕτω δὴ καὶ ψυχῇ προηγουμένως
μὲν καρπὸς ἡ ἀλήθεια, οὐκ ἄχαρί γε μὴν οὐδὲ τὴν θύραθεν
σοφίαν περιβεβλῆσθαι, οἷόν τινα φύλλα σκέπην τε τῷ 1o
καρπῷ καὶ ὄψιν οὐκ ἄωρον παρεχόμενα. Λέγεται τοίνυν
καὶ Μωϋσῆς ἐκεῖνος ὁ πάνυ, οὗ μέγιστόν ἐστιν ἐπὶ σοφίᾳ

παρὰ πᾶσιν ἀνθρώποις ὄνομα, τοῖς Αἰγυπτίων μαθήμασιν ἐγγυμνασάμενος τὴν διάνοιαν, οὕτω προσελθεῖν τῇ θεωρίᾳ τοῦ ὄντος. Παραπλησίως δὲ τούτῳ, κἂν τοῖς κάτω 15 χρόνοις, τὸν σοφὸν Δανιὴλ ἐπὶ Βαβυλῶνός φασι τὴν Χαλδαίων σοφίαν καταμαθόντα, τότε τῶν θείων ἅψασθαι παιδευμάτων.

IV ᾽Αλλ᾽ ὅτι μὲν οὐκ ἄχρηστον ψυχαῖς μαθήματα τὰ ἔξωθεν δὴ ταῦτα ἱκανῶς εἴρηται· ὅπως γε μὴν αὐτῶν μεθεκτέον ὑμῖν ἑξῆς ἂν εἴη λέγειν. Πρῶτον μὲν οὖν τοῖς παρὰ τῶν ποιητῶν, ἵν᾽ ἐντεῦθεν ἄρξωμαι, ἐπεὶ παντοδαποί τινές εἰσι κατὰ τοὺς λόγους, μὴ πᾶσιν ἐφεξῆς προσέχειν 5 τὸν νοῦν, ἀλλ᾽ ὅταν μὲν τὰς τῶν ἀγαθῶν ἀνδρῶν πράξεις ἢ λόγους ὑμῖν διεξίωσιν, ἀγαπᾶν τε καὶ ζηλοῦν, καὶ ὅτι μάλιστα πειρᾶσθαι τοιούτους εἶναι, ὅταν δὲ ἐπὶ μοχθηροὺς ἄνδρας ἔλθωσι τῇ μιμήσει, ταῦτα δεῖ φεύγειν ἐπιφρασσο- μένους τὰ ὦτα οὐχ ἧττον ἢ τὸν ᾽Οδυσσέα φασὶν ἐκεῖνοι 10 τὰ τῶν Σειρήνων μέλη. ῾Η γὰρ πρὸς τοὺς φαύλους τῶν λόγων συνήθεια ὁδός τίς ἐστιν ἐπὶ τὰ πράγματα. Διὸ δὴ πάσῃ φυλακῇ τὴν ψυχὴν τηρητέον, μὴ διὰ τῆς τῶν λόγων ἡδονῆς παραδεξάμενοί τι λάθωμεν τῶν χειρόνων, ὥσπερ οἱ τὰ δηλητήρια μετὰ τοῦ μέλιτος προσιέμενοι. Οὐ τοίνυν 15 ⟨ἐν πᾶσιν⟩ ἐπαινεσόμεθα τοὺς ποιητάς, οὐ λοιδορουμένους, οὐ σκώπτοντας, οὐκ ἐρῶντας ἢ μεθύοντας μιμουμένους, οὐχ ὅταν τραπέζῃ πληθούσῃ καὶ ᾠδαῖς ἀνειμέναις τὴν εὐδαιμονίαν ὁρίζωνται. Πάντων δὲ ἥκιστα περὶ θεῶν τι διαλεγομένοις προσέξομεν, καὶ μάλισθ᾽ ὅταν ὡς περὶ 20 πολλῶν τε αὐτῶν διεξίωσι καὶ τούτων οὐδ᾽ ὁμονοούντων. ᾽Αδελφὸς γὰρ δὴ παρ᾽ ἐκείνοις διαστασιάζει πρὸς ἀδελφόν, καὶ γονεὺς πρὸς παῖδας, καὶ τούτοις αὖθις πρὸς τοὺς τεκόντας πόλεμός ἐστιν ἀκήρυκτος. Μοιχείας δὲ θεῶν καὶ ἔρωτας καὶ μίξεις ἀναφανδόν, καὶ ταύτας γε μάλιστα τοῦ 25 κορυφαίου πάντων καὶ ὑπάτου Διός, ὡς αὐτοὶ λέγουσιν, ἃ κἂν περὶ βοσκημάτων τις λέγων ἐρυθριάσειε, τοῖς ἐπὶ

22

σκηνῆς καταλείψομεν. Ταὐτὰ δὴ ταῦτα λέγειν καὶ περὶ
συγγραφέων ἔχω, καὶ μάλισθ' ὅταν ψυχαγωγίας ἕνεκα τῶν
ἀκουόντων λογοποιῶσι. Καὶ ῥητόρων δὲ τὴν περὶ τὸ ψεύ- 30
δεσθαι τέχνην οὐ μιμησόμεθα. Οὔτε γὰρ ἐν δικαστηρίοις,
οὔτ' ἐν ταῖς ἄλλαις πράξεσιν ἐπιτήδειον ἡμῖν τὸ ψεῦδος,
τοῖς τὴν ὀρθὴν ὁδὸν καὶ ἀληθῆ προελομένοις τοῦ βίου, οἷς
τὸ μὴ δικάζεσθαι νόμῳ προστεταγμένον ἐστίν. Ἀλλ' ἐκεῖνα
αὐτῶν μᾶλλον ἀποδεξόμεθα, ἐν οἷς ἀρετὴν ἐπῄνεσαν ἢ 35
πονηρίαν διέβαλον. Ὡς γὰρ τῶν ἀνθέων τοῖς μὲν λοιποῖς
ἄχρι τῆς εὐωδίας ἢ τῆς χρόας ἐστὶν ἡ ἀπόλαυσις, ταῖς
μελίτταις δ' ἄρα καὶ μέλι λαμβάνειν ἀπ' αὐτῶν ὑπάρχει,
οὕτω δὴ κἀνταῦθα τοῖς μὴ τὸ ἡδὺ καὶ ἐπίχαρι μόνον τῶν
τοιούτων λόγων διώκουσιν ἔστι τινὰ καὶ ὠφέλειαν ἀπ' 40
αὐτῶν εἰς τὴν ψυχὴν ἀποθέσθαι. Κατὰ πᾶσαν δὴ οὖν τῶν
μελιττῶν τὴν εἰκόνα τῶν λόγων ἡμῖν μεθεκτέον. Ἐκεῖναί
τε γὰρ οὔτε ἅπασι τοῖς ἄνθεσι παραπλησίως ἐπέρχονται,
οὔτε μὴν οἷς ἂν ἐπιπτῶσιν ὅλα φέρειν ἐπιχειροῦσιν, ἀλλ'
ὅσον αὐτῶν ἐπιτήδειον πρὸς τὴν ἐργασίαν λαβοῦσαι, τὸ 45
λοιπὸν χαίρειν ἀφῆκαν· ἡμεῖς τε, ἢν σωφρονῶμεν, ὅσον
οἰκεῖον ἡμῖν καὶ συγγενὲς τῇ ἀληθείᾳ παρ' αὐτῶν κομισά-
μενοι, ὑπερβησόμεθα τὸ λειπόμενον. Καὶ καθάπερ τῆς
ῥοδωνιᾶς τοῦ ἄνθους δρεψάμενοι τὰς ἀκάνθας ἐκκλίνομεν,
οὕτω καὶ ἐπὶ τῶν τοιούτων λόγων ὅσον χρήσιμον καρπωσά- 50
μενοι, τὸ βλαβερὸν φυλαξώμεθα. Εὐθὺς οὖν ἐξ ἀρχῆς
ἐπισκοπεῖν ἕκαστον τῶν μαθημάτων, καὶ συναρμόζειν τῷ
τέλει προσήκε, κατὰ τὴν Δωρικὴν παροιμίαν, τὸν λίθον
ποτὶ τὰν σπάρτον ἄγοντας.

V Καὶ ἐπειδήπερ δι' ἀρετῆς ἐπὶ τὸν βίον ἡμῖν καθεῖναι·
δεῖ τὸν ἡμέτερον, εἰς ταύτην δὲ πολλὰ μὲν ποιηταῖς, πολλὰ
δὲ συγγραφεῦσι, πολλῷ δὲ ἔτι πλείω φιλοσόφοις ἀνδράσιν
ὕμνηται, τοῖς τοιούτοις τῶν λόγων μάλιστα προσεκτέον.
Οὐ μικρὸν γὰρ τὸ ὄφελος, οἰκειότητά τινα καὶ συνήθειαν 5
ταῖς τῶν νέων ψυχαῖς τῆς ἀρετῆς ἐγγενέσθαι· ἐπείπερ

4

23

ἀμετάστατα πέφυκεν εἶναι τὰ τῶν τοιούτων μαθήματα, δι᾽ ἀπαλότητα τῶν ψυχῶν εἰς βάθος ἐνσημαινόμενα. Ἢ τί ποτε ἄλλο διανοηθέντα τὸν Ἡσίοδον ὑπολάβωμεν ταυτὶ ποιῆσαι τὰ ἔπη ἃ πάντες ᾄδουσιν, ἢ οὐχὶ προτρέποντα 10 τοὺς νέους ἐπ᾽ ἀρετήν; Ὅτι τραχεῖα μὲν πρῶτον καὶ δύσβατος καὶ ἱδρῶτος συχνοῦ καὶ πόνου πλήρης ἡ πρὸς ἀρετὴν φέρουσα καὶ ἀνάντης ὁδός. Διόπερ οὐ παντὸς οὔτε προσβῆναι αὐτῇ διὰ τὸ ὄρθιον, οὔτε προσβάντα ῥᾳδίως ἐπὶ τὸ ἄκρον ἐλθεῖν. Ἄνω δὲ γενομένῳ ὁρᾶν ὑπάρχει ὡς μὲν 15 λεία τε καὶ καλή, ὡς δὲ ῥᾳδία τε καὶ εὔπορος, καὶ τῆς ἑτέρας ἡδίων τῆς ἐπὶ τὴν κακίαν ἀγούσης, ἣν ἀθρόον εἶναι λαβεῖν ἐκ τοῦ σύνεγγυς ὁ αὐτὸς οὗτος ποιητὴς ἔφησεν. Ἐμοὶ μὲν γὰρ δοκεῖ οὐδὲν ἕτερον ἢ προτρέπων ἡμᾶς ἐπ᾽ ἀρετήν, καὶ προκαλούμενος ἅπαντας ἀγαθοὺς εἶναι, ταῦτα 20 διελθεῖν καὶ ὥστε μὴ καταμαλακισθέντας πρὸς τοὺς πόνους προαποστῆναι τοῦ τέλους. Καὶ μέντοι, καὶ εἴ τις ἕτερος ἐοικότα τούτοις τὴν ἀρετὴν ὕμνησεν, ὡς εἰς ταὐτὸν ἡμῖν φέροντας τοὺς λόγους ἀποδεχώμεθα.

Ὡς δ᾽ ἐγώ τινος ἤκουσα δεινοῦ καταμαθεῖν ἀνδρὸς 25 ποιητοῦ διάνοιαν, πᾶσα μὲν ἡ ποίησις τῷ Ὁμήρῳ ἀρετῆς ἐστιν ἔπαινος, καὶ πάντα αὐτῷ πρὸς τοῦτο φέρει, ὅ τι μὴ πάρεργον· οὐχ ἥκιστα δὲ ἐν οἷς τὸν στρατηγὸν τῶν Κεφαλλήνων πεποίηκε γυμνὸν ἐκ τοῦ ναυαγίου περισωθέντα· πρῶτον μὲν αἰδέσαι τὴν βασιλίδα φανέντα μόνον, 30 τοσούτου δεῖν αἰσχύνην ὀφλῆσαι γυμνὸν ὀφθέντα, ἐπειδήπερ αὐτὸν ἀρετῇ ἀντὶ ἱματίων κεκοσμημένον ἐποίησε· ἔπειτα μέντοι καὶ τοῖς λοιποῖς Φαίαξι τοσούτου ἄξιον νομισθῆναι ὥστε ἀφέντας τὴν τρυφὴν ᾗ συνέζων, ἐκεῖνον ἀποβλέπειν καὶ ζηλοῦν ἅπαντας, καὶ μηδένα Φαιάκων ἐν 35 τῷ τότε εἶναι ἄλλο τι ἂν εὔξασθαι μᾶλλον ἢ Ὀδυσσέα γενέσθαι, καὶ ταῦτα ἐκ ναυαγίου περισωθέντα. Ἐν τούτοις γὰρ ἔλεγεν ὁ τοῦ ποιητοῦ τῆς διανοίας ἐξηγητὴς μονονουχὶ βοῶντα λέγειν τὸν Ὅμηρον ὅτι· Ἀρετῆς ὑμῖν ἐπιμελητέον, ὦ ἄνθρωποι, ἣ καὶ ναυαγήσαντι συνεκνήχεται καὶ ἐπὶ τῆς 40

24

χέρσου γενόμενον γυμνὸν τιμιώτερον ἀποδείξει τῶν εὐδαι-
μόνων Φαιάκων. Καὶ γὰρ οὕτως ἔχει. Τὰ μὲν ἄλλα τῶν
κτημάτων οὐ μᾶλλον τῶν ἐχόντων ἢ καὶ οὑτινοσοῦν τῶν
ἐπιτυχόντων ἐστίν, ὥσπερ ἐν παιδιᾷ κύβων τῇδε κἀκεῖσε
μεταβαλλόμενα· μόνη δὲ κτημάτων ἡ ἀρετὴ ἀναφαίρετον, 45
καὶ ζῶντι καὶ τελευτήσαντι παραμένουσα. Ὅθεν δὴ καὶ
Σόλων μοι δοκεῖ πρὸς τοὺς εὐπόρους εἰπεῖν τό·

ἈΑλλ' ἡμεῖς αὐτοῖς οὐ διαμειψόμεθα
τῆς ἀρετῆς τὸν πλοῦτον· ἐπεὶ τὸ μὲν ἔμπεδον αἰεί,
χρήματα δ' ἀνθρώπων ἄλλοτε ἄλλος ἔχει.   50

Παραπλήσια δὲ τούτοις καὶ τὰ Θεόγνιδος, ἐν οἷς φησι
τὸν θεόν, ὅντινα δὴ καί φησι, τοῖς ἀνθρώποις τὸ τάλαντον
ἐπιρρέπειν ἄλλοτε ἄλλως, « ἄλλοτε μὲν πλουτεῖν, ἄλλοτε
δὲ μηδὲν ἔχειν ».

Καὶ μὴν καὶ ὁ Κεῖός που σοφιστὴς τῶν ἑαυτοῦ συγγραμ- 55
μάτων ἀδελφὰ τούτοις εἰς ἀρετὴν καὶ κακίαν ἐφιλοσό-
φησεν· ᾧ δὴ καὶ αὐτῷ τὴν διάνοιαν προσεκτέον· οὐ γὰρ
ἀπόβλητος ὁ ἀνήρ. Ἔχει δὲ οὕτω πως ὁ λόγος αὐτῷ, ὅσα
ἐγὼ τοῦ ἀνδρὸς τῆς διανοίας μέμνημαι, ἐπεὶ τά γε ῥήματα
οὐκ ἐπίσταμαι, πλήν γε δὴ ὅτι ἁπλῶς οὕτως εἴρηκεν 60
ἄνευ μέτρου· ὅτι νέῳ ὄντι τῷ Ἡρακλεῖ κομιδῇ, καὶ
σχεδὸν ταύτην ἄγοντι τὴν ἡλικίαν, ἣν καὶ ὑμεῖς νῦν,
βουλευομένῳ ποτέραν τράπηται τῶν ὁδῶν, τὴν διὰ τῶν
πόνων ἄγουσαν πρὸς ἀρετήν, ἢ τὴν ῥᾴστην, προσελθεῖν
δύο γυναῖκας, ταύτας δὲ εἶναι Ἀρετὴν καὶ Κακίαν. Εὐθὺς 65
μὲν οὖν καὶ σιωπώσας ἐμφαίνειν ἀπὸ τοῦ σχήματος τὸ
διάφορον. Εἶναι γὰρ τὴν μὲν ὑπὸ κομμωτικῆς διεσκευασ-
μένην εἰς κάλλος, καὶ ὑπὸ τρυφῆς διαρρεῖν, καὶ πάντα
ἑσμὸν ἡδονῆς ἐξηρτημένην ἄγειν· ταῦτά τε οὖν δεικνύναι,
καὶ ἔτι πλείω τούτων ὑπισχνουμένην, ἕλκειν ἐπιχειρεῖν 70
τὸν Ἡρακλέα πρὸς ἑαυτήν· τὴν δ' ἑτέραν κατεσκληκέναι,
καὶ αὐχμεῖν, καὶ σύντονον βλέπειν, καὶ λέγειν τοιαῦτα
ἕτερα· ὑπισχνεῖσθαι γὰρ οὐδὲν ἀνειμένον, οὐδὲ ἡδύ, ἀλλ'

25

ἱδρῶτας μυρίους καὶ πόνους καὶ κινδύνους, διὰ πάσης
ἠπείρου τε καὶ θαλάσσης, ἆθλον δὲ τούτων εἶναι θεὸν 75
γενέσθαι, ὡς ὁ ἐκείνου λόγος· ᾗπερ δὴ καὶ τελευτῶντα τὸν
Ἡρακλέα συνέπεσθαι.

VI Καὶ σχεδὸν ἅπαντες ὧν δὴ καὶ λόγος τίς ἐστιν ἐπὶ
σοφίᾳ, ἢ μικρὸν ἢ μεῖζον εἰς δύναμιν ἕκαστος ἐν τοῖς
ἑαυτῶν συγγράμμασιν ἀρετῆς ἔπαινον διεξῆλθον· οἷς πειστέον καὶ πειρατέον ἐπὶ τοῦ βίου δεικνύναι τοὺς λόγους.
Ὡς ὅ γε τὴν ἄχρι ῥημάτων παρὰ τοῖς ἄλλοις φιλοσοφίαν 5
ἔργῳ βεβαιῶν

οἷος πέπνυται· τοὶ δὲ σκιαὶ ἀΐσσουσι.

Καί μοι δοκεῖ τὸ τοιοῦτον παραπλήσιον εἶναι ὥσπερ ἂν
εἰ ζωγράφου θαυμαστόν τι οἷον κάλλος ἀνθρώπου μιμησαμένου, ὁ δὲ αὐτὸς εἴη τοιοῦτος ἐπὶ τῆς ἀληθείας οἷον ἐπὶ 10
τῶν πινάκων ἐκεῖνος ἔδειξεν. Ἐπεὶ τό γε λαμπρῶς μὲν
ἐπαινέσαι τὴν ἀρετὴν εἰς τὸ μέσον, καὶ μακροὺς ὑπὲρ
αὐτῆς ἀποτείνειν λόγους, ἰδίᾳ δὲ τὸ ἡδὺ πρὸ τῆς σωφρο-
σύνης, καὶ τὸ πλέον ἔχειν πρὸ τοῦ δικαίου τιμᾶν, ἐοικέναι
φαίην ἂν ἔγωγε τοῖς ἐπὶ σκηνῆς ὑποκρινομένοις τὰ 15
δράματα· οἳ ὡς βασιλεῖς καὶ δυνάσται πολλάκις εἰσέρ-
χονται, οὔτε βασιλεῖς ὄντες, οὔτε δυνάσται, οὐδὲ μὲν οὖν
τυχὸν ἐλεύθεροι τὸ παράπαν. Εἶτα μουσικὸς μὲν οὐκ ἂν
ἑκὼν δέξαιτο ἀνάρμοστον αὐτῷ τὴν λύραν εἶναι, καὶ χοροῦ
κορυφαῖος μὴ ὅτι μάλιστα συνᾴδοντα τὸν χορὸν ἔχειν· 20
αὐτὸς δέ τις ἕκαστος διαστασιάσει πρὸς ἑαυτόν, καὶ οὐχὶ
τοῖς λόγοις ὁμολογοῦντα τὸν βίον παρέξεται; ἀλλ᾽ « ἡ
γλῶττα μὲν ὀμώμοκεν, ἡ δὲ φρὴν ἀνώμοτος » κατ᾽ Εὐρι-
πίδην ἐρεῖ; καὶ τὸ δοκεῖν ἀγαθὸς πρὸ τοῦ εἶναι διώξεται;
Ἀλλ᾽ οὗτός ἐστιν ὁ ἔσχατος τῆς ἀδικίας ὅρος, εἴ τι δεῖ 25
Πλάτωνι πείθεσθαι, τὸ δοκεῖν δίκαιον εἶναι μὴ ὄντα.

VII Τοὺς μὲν οὖν τῶν λόγων οἳ τὰς τῶν καλῶν ἔχουσιν

ὑποθήκας, οὕτως ἀποδεχώμεθα. Ἐπειδὴ δὲ καὶ πράξεις σπουδαῖαι τῶν παλαιῶν ἀνδρῶν ἢ μνήμης ἀκολουθίᾳ πρὸς ἡμᾶς διασώζονται, ἢ ποιητῶν ἢ συγγραφέων φυλαττόμεναι λόγοις, μηδὲ τῆς ἐντεῦθεν ὠφελείας ἀπολειπώμεθα. Οἷον, 5 ἐλοιδόρει τὸν Περικλέα τῶν ἐξ ἀγορᾶς τις ἀνθρώπων· ὁ δὲ οὐ προσεῖχε· καὶ εἰς πᾶσαν διήρκεσαν τὴν ἡμέραν, ὁ μὲν ἀφειδῶς πλύνων αὐτὸν τοῖς ὀνείδεσιν, ὁ δὲ οὐ μέλον αὐτῷ. Εἶτα, ἑσπέρας ἤδη καὶ σκότους, ἀπαλλαττόμενον μόλις ὑπὸ φωτὶ παρέπεμψε Περικλῆς, ὅπως αὐτῷ μὴ 10 διαφθαρείη τὸ πρὸς φιλοσοφίαν γυμνάσιον. Πάλιν τις Εὐκλείδῃ τῷ Μεγαρόθεν παροξυνθεὶς θάνατον ἠπείλησε καὶ ἐπώμοσεν· ὁ δὲ ἀντώμοσεν ἦ μὴν ἱλεώσασθαι αὐτὸν καὶ παύσειν χαλεπῶς πρὸς αὐτὸν ἔχοντα. Πόσου ἄξιον τῶν τοιούτων τι παραδειγμάτων εἰσελθεῖν τὴν μνήμην ἀνδρὸς 15 ὑπὸ ὀργῆς ἤδη κατεχομένου; Τῇ τραγῳδίᾳ γὰρ οὐ πιστευτέον « ἁπλῶς » λεγούσῃ « ἐπ᾽ ἐχθροὺς θυμὸς ὁπλίζει χέρα », ἀλλὰ μάλιστα μὲν μηδὲ διανίστασθαι πρὸς θυμὸν τὸ παράπαν, εἰ δὲ μὴ ῥᾴδιον τοῦτο, ἀλλ᾽ ὥσπερ χαλινὸν αὐτῷ τὸν λογισμὸν ἐμβάλλοντας, μὴ ἐᾶν ἐκφέρεσθαι περαι- 20 τέρω.

Ἐπαναγάγωμεν δὲ τὸν λόγον αὖθις πρὸς τὰ τῶν σπουδαίων πράξεων παραδείγματα. Ἔτυπτέ τις τὸν Σωφρονίσκου Σωκράτην εἰς αὐτὸ τὸ πρόσωπον ἐμπεσὼν ἀφειδῶς· ὁ δὲ οὐκ ἀντῆρεν, ἀλλὰ παρεῖχε τῷ παροινοῦντι 25 τῆς ὀργῆς ἐμφορεῖσθαι, ὥστε ἐξοιδεῖν ἤδη καὶ ὕπουλον αὐτῷ τὸ πρόσωπον ὑπὸ τῶν πληγῶν εἶναι. Ὡς δ᾽ οὖν ἐπαύσατο τύπτων, ἄλλο μὲν οὐδὲν ὁ Σωκράτης ποιῆσαι, ἐπιγράψαι δὲ τῷ μετώπῳ λέγεται, ὥσπερ ἀνδριάντι τὸν δημιουργόν, ὁ δεῖνα ἐποίει· καὶ τοσοῦτον ἀμύνασθαι. 30 Ταῦτα σχεδὸν εἰς ταὐτὸν τοῖς ἡμετέροις φέροντα πολλοῦ ἄξιον εἶναι μιμήσασθαι τοὺς τηλικούτους φημί. Τουτὶ μὲν γὰρ τὸ τοῦ Σωκράτους ἀδελφὸν ἐκείνῳ τῷ παραγγέλματι, ὅτι τῷ τύπτοντι κατὰ τῆς σιαγόνος καὶ τὴν ἑτέραν παρέχειν προσῆκε, τοσούτου δεῖν ἀπαμύνασθαι, τὸ δὲ τοῦ 35

Περικλέους ἢ τὸ Εὐκλείδου τῷ τοὺς διώκοντας ὑπομένειν καὶ πράως αὐτῶν τῆς ὀργῆς ἀνέχεσθαι, καὶ τῷ τοῖς ἐχθροῖς εὔχεσθαι τὰ ἀγαθά, ἀλλὰ μὴ ἐπαρᾶσθαι. Ὡς ὅ γε ἐν τούτοις προπαιδευθεὶς οὐκ ἔτ᾽ ἂν ἐκείνοις ὡς ἀδυνάτοις διαπιστήσειεν. Οὐδ᾽ ἂν παρέλθοιμι τὸ τοῦ Ἀλεξάνδρου, ὃς 40 τὰς θυγατέρας Δαρείου αἰχμαλώτους λαβὼν θαυμαστόν τι οἶον τὸ κάλλος παρέχειν μαρτυρουμένας οὐδὲ προσιδεῖν ἠξίωσεν, αἰσχρὸν εἶναι κρίνων τὸν ἄνδρας ἑλόντα γυναικῶν ἡττηθῆναι. Τουτὶ γὰρ εἰς ταὐτὸν ἐκείνῳ φέρει, ὅτι ὁ ἐμβλέψας πρὸς ἡδονὴν γυναικί, κἂν μὴ τῷ ἔργῳ τὴν 45 μοιχείαν ἐπιτελέσῃ, ἀλλὰ τῷ γε τὴν ἐπιθυμίαν τῇ ψυχῇ παραδέξασθαι, οὐκ ἀφίεται τοῦ ἐγκλήματος. Τὸ δὲ τοῦ Κλεινίου, τῶν Πυθαγόρου γνωρίμων ἑνός, χαλεπὸν πιστεῦσαι ἀπὸ ταὐτομάτου συμβῆναι τοῖς ἡμετέροις, ἀλλ᾽ οὐχὶ μιμησαμένου σπουδῇ. Τί δὲ ἦν ὃ ἐποίησεν ἐκεῖνος; Ἐξὸν 50 δι᾽ ὅρκου τριῶν ταλάντων ζημίαν ἀποφυγεῖν, ὃ δὲ ἀπέτισε μᾶλλον ἢ ὤμοσε, καὶ ταῦτα εὐορκεῖν μέλλων, ἀκούσας ἐμοὶ δοκεῖν τοῦ προστάγματος τὸν ὅρκον ἡμῖν ἀπαγορεύοντος.

VIII Ἀλλ᾽, ὅπερ ἐξ ἀρχῆς ἔλεγον, πάλιν γὰρ εἰς ταὐτὸν ἐπανίωμεν, οὐ πάντα ἐφεξῆς παραδεκτέον ἡμῖν, ἀλλ᾽ ὅσα χρήσιμα. Καὶ γὰρ αἰσχρὸν τῶν μὲν σιτίων τὰ βλαβερὰ διωθεῖσθαι, τῶν δὲ μαθημάτων ἃ τὴν ψυχὴν ἡμῶν τρέφει μηδένα λόγον ἔχειν, ἀλλ᾽ ὥσπερ χειμάρρουν παρασύροντας 5 ἅπαν τὸ προστυχὸν ἐμβάλλεσθαι. Καίτοι τίνα ἔχει λόγον, κυβερνήτην μὲν οὐκ εἰκῇ τοῖς πνεύμασιν ἐφιέναι, ἀλλὰ πρὸς ὅρμους εὐθύνειν τὸ σκάφος, καὶ τοξότην κατὰ σκοποῦ βάλλειν, καὶ μὲν δὴ καὶ χαλκευτικόν τινα ἢ τεκτονικὸν ὄντα τοῦ κατὰ τὴν τέχνην ἐφίεσθαι τέλους, ἡμᾶς δὲ 10 καὶ τῶν τοιούτων δημιουργῶν ἀπολείπεσθαι, πρός γε τὸ συνορᾶν δύνασθαι τὰ ἡμέτερα; Οὐ γὰρ δὴ τῶν μὲν χειρωνακτῶν ἔστί τι πέρας τῆς ἐργασίας, τοῦ δὲ ἀνθρωπίνου βίου σκοπὸς οὐκ ἔστι, πρὸς ὃν ἀφορῶντα πάντα ποιεῖν καὶ λέγειν χρὴ τόν γε μὴ τοῖς ἀλόγοις παντάπασι προσεοικέναι 15

μέλλοντα· ἢ οὕτως ἂν εἴημεν ἀτεχνῶς κατὰ τῶν πλοίων τὰ
ἀνερμάτιστα, οὐδενὸς ἡμῖν νοῦ ἐπὶ τῶν τῆς ψυχῆς οἰάκων
καθεζομένου, εἰκῇ κατὰ τὸν βίον ἄνω καὶ κάτω περιφερό-
μενοι. Ἀλλ᾽ ὥσπερ ἐν τοῖς γυμνικοῖς ἀγῶσιν, εἰ δὲ βούλει,
τοῖς μουσικῆς, ἐκείνων εἰσὶ τῶν ἀγώνων αἱ μελέται ὧνπερ 20
οἱ στέφανοι, καὶ οὐδείς γε πάλην ἀσκῶν ἢ παγκράτιον εἶτα
κιθαρίζειν ἢ αὐλεῖν μελετᾷ. Οὔκουν ὁ Πολυδάμας γε, ἀλλ᾽
ἐκεῖνος πρὸ τοῦ ἀγῶνος τοῦ Ὀλυμπίασι τὰ ἅρματα ἵστη
τρέχοντα, καὶ διὰ τούτων τὴν ἰσχὺν ἐκράτυνε. Καὶ ὁ γε
Μίλων ἀπὸ τῆς ἀληλειμμένης ἀσπίδος οὐκ ἐξωθεῖτο, ἀλλ᾽ 25
ἀντεῖχεν ὠθούμενος οὐχ ἧττον ἢ οἱ ἀνδριάντες οἱ τῷ
μολύβδῳ συνδεδεμένοι. Καὶ ἁπαξαπλῶς αἱ μελέται αὐτοῖς
παρασκευαὶ τῶν ἄθλων ἦσαν. Εἰ δὲ τὰ Μαρσύου ἢ τὰ
Ὀλύμπου τῶν Φρυγῶν περιειργάζοντο κρούματα, καταλι-
πόντες τὴν κόνιν καὶ τὰ γυμνάσια, ταχύ γ᾽ ἂν στεφάνων ἢ 30
δόξης ἔτυχον, ἢ διέφυγον τὸ μὴ καταγέλαστοι εἶναι κατὰ
τὸ σῶμα. Ἀλλ᾽ οὐ μέντοι οὐδ᾽ ὁ Τιμόθεος τὴν μελῳδίαν
ἀφεὶς ἐν ταῖς παλαίστραις διῆγεν. Οὐ γὰρ ἂν τοσοῦτον
ὑπῆρξεν αὐτῷ διενεγκεῖν ἁπάντων τῇ μουσικῇ, ᾧ γε
τοσοῦτον περιῆν τῆς τέχνης ὥστε καὶ θυμὸν ἐγείρειν διὰ 35
τῆς συντόνου καὶ αὐστηρᾶς ἁρμονίας, καὶ μέντοι καὶ
χαλᾶν καὶ μαλάττειν πάλιν διὰ τῆς ἀνειμένης, ὁπότε βούλοιτο. Ταύτῃ τοι καὶ Ἀλεξάνδρῳ ποτὲ τὸ Φρύγιον ἐπαυλήσαντα ἐξαναστῆσαι αὐτὸν ἐπὶ τὰ ὅπλα λέγεται μεταξὺ
δειπνοῦντα, καὶ ἐπαναγαγεῖν πάλιν πρὸς τοὺς συμπότας, 40
τὴν ἁρμονίαν χαλάσαντα. Τοσαύτην ἰσχὺν ἔν τε μουσικῇ
καὶ τοῖς γυμνικοῖς ἀγῶσι πρὸς τὴν τοῦ τέλους κτῆσιν ἡ
μελέτη παρέχεται.

Ἐπεὶ δὲ στεφάνων καὶ ἀθλητῶν ἐμνήσθην, ἐκεῖνοι
μυρία παθόντες ἐπὶ μυρίοις, καὶ πολλαχόθεν τὴν ῥώμην 45
ἑαυτοῖς συναυξήσαντες, πολλὰ μὲν γυμναστικοῖς ἐνιδρώσαντες πόνοις, πολλὰς δὲ πληγὰς ἐν παιδοτρίβου λαβόντες,
δίαιταν δὲ οὐ τὴν ἡδίστην, ἀλλὰ τὴν παρὰ τῶν γυμναστῶν
αἱρούμενοι, καὶ τἄλλα, ἵνα μὴ διατρίβω λέγων, οὕτω

διάγοντες ὡς τὸν πρὸ τῆς ἀγωνίας βίον μελέτην εἶναι τῆς 50
ἀγωνίας, τηνικαῦτα ἀποδύονται πρὸς τὸ στάδιον, καὶ
πάντα πονοῦσι καὶ κινδυνεύουσιν, ὥστε κοτίνου λαβεῖν
στέφανον ἢ σελίνου, ἢ ἄλλου τινὸς τῶν τοιούτων, καὶ
νικῶντες ἀναρρηθῆναι παρὰ τοῦ κήρυκος. Ἡμῖν δέ, οἷς
ἆθλα τοῦ βίου πρόκειται οὕτω θαυμαστὰ πλήθει. τε καὶ 55
μεγέθει ὥστε ἀδύνατα εἶναι ῥηθῆναι λόγῳ, ἐπ᾿ ἄμφω
καθεύδουσι, καὶ κατὰ πολλὴν διαιτωμένοις ἄδειαν, τῇ ἑτέρᾳ
λαβεῖν τῶν χειρῶν ὑπάρξει; Πολλοῦ μέντ᾿ ἂν ἄξιον ἦν ἡ
ῥαθυμία τῷ βίῳ, καὶ ὅ γε Σαρδανάπαλος τὰ πρῶτα πάντων·
εἰς εὐδαιμονίαν ἐφέρετο, ἢ καὶ ὁ Μαργίτης, εἰ βούλει, ὃν 60
οὔτ᾿ ἀροτῆρα, οὔτε σκαπτῆρα, οὔτε ἄλλο τι τῶν κατὰ τὸν
βίον ἐπιτήδειον εἶναι Ὅμηρος ἔφησεν, εἰ δὴ Ὁμήρου
ταῦτα. Ἀλλὰ μὴ ἀληθὴς μᾶλλον ὁ τοῦ Πιττακοῦ λόγος, ὃς
χαλεπὸν ἔφησεν ἐσθλὸν ἔμμεναι; Διὰ πολλῶν γὰρ δὴ τῷ
ὄντι πόνων διεξελθοῦσι μόλις ἂν τῶν ἀγαθῶν ἐκείνων 65
τυχεῖν ἡμῖν περιγένοιτο, ὧν ἐν τοῖς ἄνω λόγοις οὐδὲν
εἶναι παράδειγμα τῶν ἀνθρωπίνων ἐλέγομεν. Οὐ δὴ οὖν
ῥαθυμητέον ἡμῖν, οὐδὲ τῆς ἐν βραχεῖ ῥᾳστώνης μεγάλας
ἐλπίδας ἀνταλλακτέον, εἴπερ μὴ μέλλοιμεν ὀνείδη τε ἕξειν
καὶ τιμωρίας ὑφέξειν, οὗ τι παρὰ τοῖς ἀνθρώποις ἐνθάδε 70
(καίτοι καὶ τοῦτο οὐ μικρὸν τῷ γε νοῦν ἔχοντι), ἀλλ᾿ ἐν
τοῖς, εἴτε ὑπὸ γῆν, εἴτε καὶ ὅπου δὴ τοῦ παντὸς ὄντα
τυγχάνει, δικαιωτηρίοις. Ὡς τῷ μὲν ἀκουσίως τοῦ προσή-
κοντος ἁμαρτόντι κἂν συγγνώμη τις ἴσως παρὰ τοῦ Θεοῦ
γένοιτο· τῷ δὲ ἐξεπίτηδες τὰ χείρω προελομένῳ οὐδε- 75
μία παραίτησις τὸ μὴ οὐχὶ πολλαπλασίω τὴν κόλασιν
ὑποσχεῖν.

IX   Τί οὖν ποιῶμεν; φαίη τις ἄν. Τί ἄλλο γε ἢ τῆς
ψυχῆς ἐπιμέλειαν ἔχειν, πᾶσαν σχολὴν ἀπὸ τῶν ἄλλων
ἄγοντας; Οὐ δὴ οὖν τῷ σώματι δουλευτέον, ὅτι μὴ πᾶσα
ἀνάγκη· ἀλλὰ τῇ ψυχῇ τὰ βέλτιστα ποριστέον, ὥσπερ ἐκ
δεσμωτηρίου τῆς πρὸς τὰ τοῦ σώματος πάθη κοινωνίας 5

30

αὐτὴν διὰ φιλοσοφίας λύοντας, ἅμα δὲ καὶ τὸ σῶμα τῶν
παθῶν κρεῖττον ἀπεργαζομένους, γαστρὶ μέν γε τὰ ἀναγ-
καῖα ὑπηρετοῦντας, οὐχὶ τὰ ἥδιστα, ὡς οἵ γε τραπεζοποιούς τινας καὶ μαγείρους περινοοῦντες, καὶ πᾶσαν
διερευνώμενοι γῆν τε καὶ θάλασσαν, οἷόν τινι χαλεπῷ 10
δεσπότῃ φόρους ἀπάγοντες, ἐλεεινοὶ τῆς ἀσχολίας, τῶν ἐν
ᾅδου κολαζομένων οὐδὲν πάσχοντες ἀνεκτότερον, ἀτεχνῶς
εἰς πῦρ ξαίνοντες, καὶ κοσκίνῳ φέροντες ὕδωρ, καὶ εἰς
τετρημένον ἀντλοῦντες πίθον, οὐδὲν πέρας τῶν πόνων
ἔχοντες. Κουρὰς δὲ καὶ ἀμπεχόνας ἔξω τῶν ἀναγκαίων 15
περιεργάζεσθαι, ἢ δυστυχούντων ἐστί, κατὰ τὸν Διογένους
λόγον, ἢ ἀδικούντων. Ὥστε καλλωπιστὴν εἶναι καὶ
ὀνομάζεσθαι ὁμοίως αἰσχρὸν ἡγεῖσθαί φημι δεῖν τοὺς
τοιούτους ὡς τὸ ἑταιρεῖν ἢ ἀλλοτρίοις γάμοις ἐπιβουλεύειν.
Τί γὰρ ἂν διαφέροι, τῷ γε νοῦν ἔχοντι, ξυστίδα ἀναβεβλῆ- 20
σθαι, ἤ τι τῶν φαύλων ἱμάτιον φέρειν, ἕως ἂν μηδὲν
ἐνδέῃ τοῦ πρὸς χειμῶνά τε εἶναι καὶ θάλπος ἀλεξητήριον ;
Καὶ τἄλλα δὴ τὸν αὐτὸν τρόπον μὴ περιττότερον τῆς
χρείας κατεσκευάσθαι, μηδὲ περιέπειν τὸ σῶμα πλέον ἢ
ὡς ἄμεινον τῇ ψυχῇ. Οὐχ ἧττον γὰρ ὄνειδος ἀνδρί, τῷ γε 25
ὡς ἀληθῶς τῆς προσηγορίας ταύτης ἀξίῳ, καλλωπιστὴν
καὶ φιλοσώματον εἶναι, ἢ πρὸς ἄλλο τι τῶν παθῶν ἀγεννῶς
διακεῖσθαι. Τὸ γὰρ τὴν πᾶσαν σπουδὴν εἰσφέρεσθαι ὅπως
ὡς κάλλιστα αὐτῷ τὸ σῶμα ἕξοι οὐ διαγινώσκοντός ἐστιν
ἑαυτόν, οὐδὲ συνιέντος τοῦ σοφοῦ παραγγέλματος, ὅτι οὐ 30
τὸ ὁρώμενόν ἐστιν ὁ ἄνθρωπος, ἀλλά τινος δεῖ περιττο-
τέρας σοφίας, δι' ἧς ἕκαστος ἡμῶν ὅστις ποτέ ἐστιν
ἑαυτὸν ἐπιγνώσεται. Τοῦτο δὲ μὴ καθηραμένοις τὸν νοῦν
ἀδυνατώτερον ἢ λημῶντι πρὸς τὸν ἥλιον ἀναβλέψαι.
Κάθαρσις δὲ ψυχῆς, ὡς ἀθρόως τε εἰπεῖν καὶ ὑμῖν ἱκανῶς, 35
τὰς διὰ τῶν αἰσθήσεων ἡδονὰς ἀτιμάζειν· μὴ ὀφθαλμοὺς
ἑστιᾶν ταῖς ἀτόποις τῶν θαυματοποιῶν ἐπιδείξεσιν, ἢ
σωμάτων θέαις ἡδονῆς κέντρον ἐναφιέντων, μὴ διὰ τῶν
ὤτων διεφθαρμένην μελῳδίαν τῶν ψυχῶν καταχεῖν· ἀνε-

31

λευθερίας γὰρ δὴ καὶ ταπεινότητος ἔκγονα πάθη ἐκ τοῦ 40
τοιοῦδε τῆς μουσικῆς εἴδους ἐγγίνεσθαι πέφυκεν. Ἀλλὰ
τὴν ἑτέραν μεταδιωκτέον ἡμῖν, τὴν ἀμείνω τε καὶ εἰς
ἄμεινον φέρουσαν, ᾗ καὶ Δαβὶδ χρώμενος, ὁ ποιητὴς τῶν
ἱερῶν ᾀσμάτων, ἐκ τῆς μανίας, ὥς φασι, τὸν βασιλέα
καθίστη. Λέγεται δὲ καὶ Πυθαγόραν, κωμασταῖς περιτυ- 45
χόντα μεθύουσι, κελεῦσαι τὸν αὐλητὴν τὸν τοῦ κώμου.
κατάρχοντα, μεταβαλόντα τὴν ἁρμονίαν, ἐπαυλῆσαί σφισι
τὸ Δώριον· τοὺς δὲ οὕτως ἀναφρονῆσαι ὑπὸ τοῦ μέλους
ὥστε τοὺς στεφάνους ῥίψαντας, αἰσχυνομένους ἐπανελθεῖν.
Ἕτεροι δὲ πρὸς αὐλὸν κορυβαντιῶσι καὶ ἐκβακχεύονται. 50
Τοσοῦτόν ἐστι τὸ διάφορον ὑγιοῦς ἢ μοχθηρᾶς μελῳδίας
ἀναπλησθῆναι. Ὥστε τῆς νῦν δὴ κρατούσης ταύτης
ἧττον ὑμῖν μεθεκτέον ἢ οὑτινοσοῦν τῶν προδήλως αἰσχίστων.
Ἀτμούς γε μὴν παντοδαποὺς ἡδονὴν ὀσφρήσει φέροντας
τῷ ἀέρι καταμιγνύναι, ἢ μύροις ἑαυτοὺς ἀναχρώννυσθαι, 55
καὶ ἀπαγορεύειν αἰσχύνομαι. Τί δ᾽ ἄν τις εἴποι περὶ τοῦ
μὴ χρῆναι τὰς ἐν ἁφῇ καὶ γεύσει διώκειν ἡδονάς, ἢ ὅτι
καταναγκάζουσιν αὗται τοὺς περὶ τὴν ἑαυτῶν θήραν
ἐσχολακότας, ὥσπερ τὰ θρέμματα, πρὸς τὴν γαστέρα καὶ
τὰ ὑπ᾽ αὐτὴν συννενευκότας ζῆν; 60
Ἑνὶ δὲ λόγῳ, παντὸς ὑπεροπτέον τοῦ σώματος τῷ μὴ
ὡς ἐν βορβόρῳ ταῖς ἡδοναῖς αὐτοῦ κατορωρύχθαι μέλλοντι,
ἢ τοσοῦτον ἀνθεκτέον αὐτοῦ ὅσον, φησὶ Πλάτων, ὑπη-
ρεσίαν φιλοσοφίᾳ κτωμένους, ἐοικότα που λέγων τῷ
Παύλῳ, ὃς παραινεῖ μηδεμίαν χρῆναι τοῦ σώματος 65
πρόνοιαν ἔχειν εἰς ἐπιθυμιῶν ἀφορμήν. Ἢ τί διαφέρουσιν
οἳ τοῦ μὲν σώματος, ὡς ἂν κάλλιστα ἔχοι, φροντίζουσι,
τὴν δὲ χρησομένην αὐτῷ ψυχὴν ὡς οὐδενὸς ἀξίαν
περιορῶσι, τῶν περὶ τὰ ὄργανα σπουδαζόντων, τῆς δὲ δι᾽
αὐτῶν ἐνεργούσης τέχνης καταμελούντων; Πᾶν μὲν οὖν 70
τοὐναντίον κολάζειν αὐτὸ καὶ κατέχειν, ὥσπερ θηρίου τὰς
ὁρμάς, προσῆκε καὶ τοὺς ἀπ᾽ αὐτοῦ θορύβους ἐγγινομένους
τῇ ψυχῇ οἱονεὶ μάστιγι τῷ λογισμῷ καθικνουμένους

κοιμίζειν, ἀλλὰ μὴ πάντα χαλινὸν ἡδονῆς ἀνέντας.
περιορᾶν τὸν νοῦν ὥσπερ ἡνίοχον ὑπὸ δυσηνίων ἵππων 75
ὕβρει φερομένων παρασυρόμενον ἄγεσθαι· καὶ τοῦ Πυθαγόρου μεμνῆσθαι, ὃς τῶν συνόντων τινὰ καταμαθὼν
γυμνασίοις τε καὶ σιτίοις ἑαυτὸν εὖ μάλα κατασαρκοῦντα·
« Οὗτος, ἔφη, οὐ παύσῃ χαλεπώτερον σεαυτῷ κατασκευά-
ζων τὸ δεσμωτήριον ; » Διὸ δὴ καὶ Πλάτωνά φασι, τὴν ἐκ 80
σώματος βλάβην προϊδόμενον, τὸ νοσῶδες χωρίον τῆς
Ἀττικῆς τὴν Ἀκαδημίαν καταλαβεῖν ἐξεπίτηδες, ἵνα τὴν
ἄγαν εὐπάθειαν τοῦ σώματος, οἷον ἀμπέλου τὴν εἰς τὰ
περιττὰ φοράν, περικόπτοι. Ἐγὼ δὲ καὶ σφαλερὰν εἶναι
τὴν ἐπ᾽ ἄκρον εὐεξίαν ἰατρῶν ἤκουσα. 85
Ὅτε τοίνυν ἡ ἄγαν αὕτη τοῦ σώματος ἐπιμέλεια αὐτῷ
τε ἀλυσιτελὴς τῷ σώματι, καὶ πρὸς τὴν ψυχὴν ἐμπόδιόν
ἐστι, τό γε ὑποπεπτωκέναι τούτῳ καὶ θεραπεύειν μανία
σαφής. Ἀλλὰ μὴν εἰ τούτου γε ὑπερορᾶν μελετήσαιμεν,
σχολῇ γ᾽ ἂν ἄλλο τι τῶν ἀνθρωπίνων θαυμάσαιμεν. Τί γὰρ 90
ἔτι χρησόμεθα πλούτῳ, τὰς διὰ τοῦ σώματος ἡδονὰς
ἀτιμάζοντες ; Ἐγὼ μὲν οὐχ ὁρῶ, πλὴν εἰ μή, κατὰ τοὺς
ἐν τοῖς μύθοις δράκοντας, ἡδονήν τινα φέροι θησαυροῖς
κατορωρυγμένοις ἐπαγρυπνεῖν. Ὅ γε μὴν ἐλευθερίως πρὸς
τὰ τοιαῦτα διακεῖσθαι πεπαιδευμένος πολλοῦ ἂν δέοι 95
ταπεινόν τι καὶ αἰσχρὸν ἔργῳ ἢ λόγῳ ποτὲ προελέσθαι. Τὸ
γὰρ τῆς χρείας περιττότερον, κἂν Λύδιον ᾖ ψῆγμα, κἂν
τῶν μυρμήκων ἔργον τῶν χρυσοφόρων, τοσούτῳ πλέον
ἀτιμάσει ὅσῳπερ ἂν ἧττον προσδέηται· αὐτὴν δὲ δήπου
τὴν χρείαν τοῖς τῆς φύσεως ἀναγκαίοις, ἀλλ᾽ οὐ ταῖς 100
ἡδοναῖς ὁριεῖται. Ὡς οἵ γε τῶν ἀναγκαίων ὅρων ἔξω
γενόμενοι, παραπλησίως τοῖς κατὰ τοῦ πρανοῦς φερο-
μένοις, πρὸς οὐδὲν στάσιμον ἔχοντες ἀποβῆναι, οὐδαμοῦ
τῆς εἰς τὸ πρόσω φορᾶς ἵστανται· ἀλλ᾽ ὅσῳπερ ἂν πλείω
προσπεριβάλωνται, τοῦ ἴσου δέονται ἢ καὶ πλείονος πρὸς 105
τὴν τῆς ἐπιθυμίας ἐκπλήρωσιν, κατὰ τὸν Ἐξηκεστίδου
Σόλωνα, ὅς φησι·

Πλούτου δ' οὐδὲν τέρμα πεφασμένον ἀνδράσι κεῖται.

Τῷ δὲ Θεόγνιδι πρὸς ταῦτα διδασκάλῳ χρηστέον λέγοντι·

Οὐκ ἔραμαι πλουτεῖν, οὔτ' εὔχομαι, ἀλλά μοι εἴη   110
Ζῆν ἀπὸ τῶν ὀλίγων, μηδὲν ἔχοντι κακόν.

Ἐγὼ δὲ καὶ Διογένους ἄγαμαι τὴν πάντων ὁμοῦ τῶν
ἀνθρωπίνων ὑπεροψίαν, ὅς γε καὶ βασιλέως τοῦ μεγάλου
ἑαυτὸν ἀπέφηνε πλουσιώτερον, τῷ ἐλαττόνων ἢ ἐκεῖνος
κατὰ τὸν βίον προσδεῖσθαι. Ἡμῖν δὲ ἄρα εἰ μὴ τὰ Πυθίου   115
τοῦ Μυσοῦ προσείη τάλαντα, καὶ πλέθρα γῆς τόσα καὶ
τόσα, καὶ βοσκημάτων ἔσμοὶ πλείους ἢ ἀριθμῆσαι, οὐδὲν
ἐξαρκέσει; Ἀλλ', οἶμαι, προσήκει ἀπόντα τε μὴ ποθεῖν
τὸν πλοῦτον, καὶ παρόντος μὴ τῷ κεκτῆσθαι μᾶλλον
φρονεῖν ἢ τῷ εἰδέναι αὐτὸν εὖ διατίθεσθαι. Τὸ γὰρ τοῦ   120
Σωκράτους εὖ ἔχει· ὃς μέγα φρονοῦντος πλουσίου ἀνδρὸς
ἐπὶ τοῖς χρήμασιν, οὐ πρότερον αὐτὸν θαυμάσειν ἔφη πρὶν
ἂν καὶ ὅτι κεχρῆσθαι τούτοις ἐπίσταται πειραθῆναι. Ἡ
Φειδίας μὲν καὶ Πολύκλειτος, εἰ τῷ χρυσίῳ μέγα ἐφρόνουν
καὶ τῷ ἐλέφαντι ὧν ὁ μὲν Ἠλείοις τὸν Δία, ὁ δὲ τὴν   125
Ἥραν Ἀργείοις ἐποιησάτην, καταγελάστω ἂν ἤστην
ἀλλοτρίῳ πλούτῳ καλλωπιζόμενοι, ἀφέντες τὴν τέχνην,
ὑφ' ἧς καὶ ὁ χρυσὸς ἡδίων καὶ τιμιώτερος ἀπεδείχθη·
ἡμεῖς δέ, τὴν ἀνθρωπείαν ἀρετὴν οὐκ ἐξαρκεῖν ἑαυτῇ πρὸς
κόσμον ὑπολαμβάνοντες, ἐλάττονος αἰσχύνης ἄξια ποιεῖν   130
οἰόμεθα;
Ἀλλὰ δῆτα πλούτου μὲν ὑπεροψόμεθα, καὶ τὰς διὰ τῶν
αἰσθήσεων ἡδονὰς ἀτιμάσομεν, κολακείας δὲ καὶ θωπείας
διωξόμεθα, καὶ τῆς Ἀρχιλόχου ἀλώπεκος τὸ κερδαλέον τε
καὶ ποικίλον ζηλώσομεν; Ἀλλ' οὐκ ἔστιν ὃ μᾶλλον   135
φευκτέον τῷ σωφρονοῦντι τοῦ πρὸς δόξαν ζῆν, καὶ τὰ τοῖς
πολλοῖς δοκοῦντα περισκοπεῖν, καὶ μὴ τὸν ὀρθὸν λόγον
ἡγεμόνα ποιεῖσθαι τοῦ βίου, ὥστε, κἂν πᾶσιν ἀνθρώποις

ἀντιλέγειν, κἂν ἀδοξεῖν καὶ κινδυνεύειν ὑπὲρ τοῦ καλοῦ δέῃ, μηδὲν αἱρεῖσθαι τῶν ὀρθῶς ἐγνωσμένων παρακινεῖν. 140 Ἢ τὸν μὴ οὕτως ἔχοντα τί τοῦ Αἰγυπτίου σοφιστοῦ φήσομεν ἀπολείπειν, ὃς φυτὸν ἐγίγνετο καὶ θηρίον, ὁπότε βούλοιτο, καὶ πῦρ καὶ ὕδωρ καὶ πάντα χρήματα, εἴπερ δὴ καὶ αὐτὸς νῦν μὲν τὸ δίκαιον ἐπαινέσεται παρὰ τοῖς τοῦτο τιμῶσι, νῦν δὲ τοὺς ἐναντίους ἀφήσει λόγους, ὅταν τὴν 145 ἀδικίαν εὐδοκιμοῦσαν αἴσθηται, ᾕπερ δίκη ἐστὶ κολάκων. Καὶ ὥσπερ φασὶ τὸν πολύποδα τὴν χρόαν πρὸς τὴν ὑποκειμένην γῆν, οὕτως αὐτὸς τὴν διάνοιαν πρὸς τὰς τῶν συνόντων γνώμας μεταβαλεῖται.

X. Ἀλλὰ ταῦτα μέν που κἂν τοῖς ἡμετέροις λόγοις τελειότερον μαθησόμεθα· ὅσον δὲ σκιαγραφίαν τινὰ τῆς ἀρετῆς, τό γε νῦν εἶναι, ἐκ τῶν ἔξωθεν παιδευμάτων περιγραψώμεθα. Τοῖς γὰρ ἐπιμελῶς ἐξ ἑκάστου τὴν ὠφέλειαν ἀθροίζουσιν, ὥσπερ τοῖς μεγάλοις τῶν ποταμῶν, 5 πολλαὶ γίνεσθαι πολλαχόθεν αἱ προσθῆκαι πεφύκασι. Τὸ γὰρ καὶ σμικρὸν ἐπὶ σμικρῷ κατατίθεσθαι, οὐ μᾶλλον εἰς ἀργυρίου προσθήκην ἢ καὶ εἰς ἡντιναοῦν ἐπιστήμην, ὀρθῶς ἔχειν ἡγεῖσθαι τῷ ποιητῇ προσῆκεν. Ὁ μὲν οὖν Βίας τῷ υἱεῖ, πρὸς Αἰγυπτίους ἀπαίροντι, καὶ πυνθανομένῳ τί ἂν 10 ποιῶν αὐτῷ μάλιστα κεχαρισμένα πράττοι· «Ἐφόδιον, ἔφη, πρὸς γῆρας κτησάμενος», τὴν ἀρετὴν δὴ τὸ ἐφόδιον λέγων, μικροῖς ὅροις αὐτὴν περιγράφων, ὅς γε ἀνθρωπίνῳ βίῳ τὴν ἀπ' αὐτῆς ὠφέλειαν ὡρίζετο. Ἐγὼ δὲ κἂν τὸ Τιθωνοῦ τις γῆρας, κἂν τὸ Ἀργανθωνίου λέγῃ, κἂν τὸ τοῦ μακροβιω- 15 τάτου παρ' ἡμῖν Μαθουσάλα, ὃς χίλια ἔτη τριάκοντα δεόντων βιῶναι λέγεται, κἂν σύμπαντα τὸν ἀφ' οὗ γεγόνασιν ἄνθρωποι χρόνον ἀναμετρῇ, ὡς ἐπὶ παίδων διανοίας γελάσομαι, εἰς τὸν μακρὸν ἀποσκοπῶν καὶ ἀγήρω αἰῶνα, οὗ πέρας οὐδὲν ἔστι τῇ ἐπινοίᾳ λαβεῖν, 20 οὗ μᾶλλόν γε ἢ τελευτὴν ὑποθέσθαι τῆς ἀθανάτου ψυχῆς. Πρὸς ὅνπερ κτᾶσθαι παραινέσαιμ' ἂν τὰ ἐφόδια, πάντα λίθον, κατὰ τὴν παροιμίαν, κινοῦντας, ὅθεν ἂν μέλλῃ τις ὑμῖν ἐπ' αὐτὸν ὠφέλεια γενήσεσθαι. Μηδ' ὅτι χαλεπὰ ταῦτα καὶ πόνου δεόμενα, διὰ τοῦτ' ἀποκνήσω- 25 μεν· ἀλλ' ἀναμνησθέντας τοῦ παραινέσαντος, ὅτι δέοι βίον μὲν ἄριστον αὐτὸν ἕκαστον προαιρεῖσθαι, ἡδὺν δὲ προσδοκᾶν τῇ συνηθείᾳ γενήσεσθαι, ἐγχειρεῖν τοῖς βελτίσ- τοις. Αἰσχρὸν γὰρ τὸν παρόντα καιρὸν προεμένους ὕστε- ρόν ποτ' ἀνακαλεῖσθαι τὸ παρελθόν, ὅτε οὐδὲν ἔσται πλέον 3ο ἀνιωμένοις.

Ἐγὼ μὲν οὖν ἃ κράτιστα εἶναι κρίνω, τὰ μὲν νῦν εἴρηκα, τὰ δὲ παρὰ πάντα τὸν βίον ὑμῖν ξυμβουλεύσω· ὑμεῖς δέ, τριῶν ἀρρωστημάτων, μὴ τῷ ἀνιάτῳ προσεοικέναι δόξητε, μηδὲ τὴν τῆς γνώμης νόσον παραπλησίαν τῇ τῶν 35 εἰς τὰ σώματα δυστυχησάντων δείξητε. Οἱ μὲν γὰρ τὰ μικρὰ τῶν παθῶν κάμνοντες, αὐτοὶ παρὰ τοὺς ἰατροὺς ἔρχονται· οἱ δὲ ὑπὸ μειζόνων καταληφθέντες ἀρρωστη- μάτων, ἐφ' ἑαυτοὺς καλοῦσι τοὺς θεραπεύσοντας· οἱ δὲ εἰς ἀνήκεστον παντελῶς μελαγχολίας παρενεχθέντες, 4ο οὐδὲ προσιόντας προσίενται. Ὃ μὴ πάθητε νῦν ὑμεῖς τοὺς ὀρθῶς ἔχοντας τῶν λογισμῶν ἀποφεύγοντες.

Commentary

The title: traditionally this essay has been called a homily and some of the manuscripts add the word ὁμιλία. Two of Boulenger's *recentiores* prefix the word λόγος, and the work evidently has something of the λόγος προτρεπτικός about it (cf. v.10). Vat. gr. 415 (10th cent.) has παραίνεσις τοῖς νέοις ὅπως κτλ., which also accords well with the general purpose of the work. —Ἑλληνικῶν: the regular term for 'pagan' in patristic and Byzantine literature.

Chapter I: B. explains the reasons which justify him in offering the advice contained in this essay to members of his family.

1. The opening phrase, which is borrowed from the opening of Demosthenes 59, exemplifies an idiomatic feature of classical Attic Greek. By a rule of word order common to many Indo-European languages an enclitic pronoun or particle (here με) becomes the second word in its clause. For an example of the same rule affecting ἄν see III.2. The rule was discovered by J. Wackernagel, *Indogermanische Forschungen* 1.1892.333–436 = *Kleine Schriften*, Göttingen 1956, 1.1–104. B. is by no means the only post-classical writer to use this idiom: see e.g. Acts 26.24 (in a rather formal speech); Lucian, *Timon* 39; Longus 1.29, 2.4, 3.16, 3.19; Menander rhetor 384.28 and 30 (p. 79 Bursian); Agathias, *proem* 11 and 4.30.

2. ξυμβουλεῦσαι can be taken as 'urge upon', as in 24 below.

3. πεπίστευκα: 'I am convinced'. The idiomatic use of the perfect to indicate a state of formed opinion is strictly unnecessary with this verb, but there is a similar expression in Demosthenes 4.51 συνοίσειν πεπεισμένος ὦ.

37

τε is correlative with τε in 8, so that the sentences describing B.'s experience and his family relationship are balanced and parallel. For the same correlative usage see IV.43, 46 and Denniston 503–4.

ἡλικίας οὕτως ἔχειν: the genitive constructed with ἔχω and an adverb is an extension of phrases such as ποῦ γῆς; and usages with μετέχω, and is common in many authors, including Plato. Cf. KG 1.382–3.

4. γεγυμνάσθαι would normally be followed by a dative, but the construction with διά is found in Philo, *De sacrificiis Abelis et Caini* 78 (1.234.15 Cohn-Wendland).

4–5. καὶ μὴν καί: this expression is very rare in classical Greek, but καὶ μήν is a common method of progressing from one item in a series to the next (Denniston 351–2, 495). Schmid 1.427, 2.307, 4.557 showed that καὶ μὴν καί is common in Lucian, Aristides and the younger Philostratus.

5. τῆς . . . . ἐπ' ἄμφω μεταβολῆς: 'vicissitudes'; the construction would have been slightly clearer if ⟨τῆς⟩ πάντα παιδευούσης followed μεταβολῆς.

6. εἶναι is otiose with πεποίηκεν. B. may have found the expression in Plato, *Gorgias* 450a1–2 (where there is a variant reading). Many analogous constructions are cited by KG1.44.

7. καθισταμένοις τὸν βίον: if the text is sound, the verb means 'begin, establish oneself in'. LSJ cite Herodotus 8.105 for the transitive use of the middle, but the text is not above suspicion (cf. J. E. Powell *ad loc.*), nor is the other passage cited by editors, Euripides *Hiketides* 522, an exact parallel. Normal Attic usage would require κ. ⟨εἰς⟩ τὸν βίον.

8. ὁδοῦ τὴν ἀσφαλεστάτην: 'the safest road'. Similar expressions are τὴν μεγίστην τῆς εὐλαβείας, Plato *Republic* 416b, μεγίστη καὶ καλλίστη τῆς φρονήσεως, *Symposium* 209. KG. 1.279–80 explain them as arising from the partitive usage τῆς γῆς (ἡ) πολλή. [Some MSS. read ὁδῶν, which must be regarded as an attempt by the copyists to simplify the construction.]

If B.'s statements in 3–8 are to be taken at their face value they suggest that he was no longer young, and in that case the work should be attributed to the last ten years of his life.

8–9. παρὰ τῆς φύσεως: he could equally well have said φυσικῇ.

For other unnecessarily elaborate prepositional phrases cf.
VIII.10, IX.83–4.

10. τυγχάνω: for this usage without the participle cf. Dodds
on Plato, *Gorgias* 502b6, where many examples from Plato
and one from Xenophon are quoted. It is amusing and somewhat surprising to find that Phrynichus, in his handbook for
the would-be writer of Attic Greek compiled in the late
second century A.D., disapproves of the omission of the participle (*Ecloge* 244).

10–11. μήτ' . . . . δέ: 'not only not . . . . but', which
would normally be expressed by μήτε . . . . τε. [Two late
MSS., Oxford Auct. T. 4.16 and Cambridge Dd. 4.16 (both
15th cent.) read τε, which may be correct; but there is no
reason to think that they have any authority, and the anacolouthon is slight enough to be easily understood.]

10. πατέρων: 'parents', a usage recognized by the lexicographer Pollux (3.8), a contemporary of Phrynichus. LSJ
cite only Hellenistic examples. ⟨τῶν⟩ πατέρων 'your parents'
might have been expected. Alternatively one could tr.
'fathers', which would be a specific indication that B. is
addressing the children of more than one of his nine brothers
and sisters.

13. δέχοισθε: the optative indicates a mixture of courtesy
and diffidence.

14–20. B. paraphrases Hesiod, *Works and days* 293ff., which
he expects his nephews to have read; δηλονότι in 16 is empha-
tic, and he could have said που if he were less sure.

14. The word order, by which τάξεως is so far removed from
τῆς δευτέρας, is artificial and results in a poor clausula.

15. δυσχερές is Attic in the sense of 'disagreeable' as here, cf.
LSJ. B. may well have in mind the expression in Demosthenes
18.3 οὐ βούλομαι δυσχερὲς εἰπεῖν οὐδὲν ἀρχόμενος τοῦ λόγου.

20. μὴ θαυμάζετε: if B. had understood the difference between present and aorist aspects he would have written μὴ
θαυμάσητε (the reading of MSS. Oxford Auct. T. 4.16 and
Cambridge Dd. 4.16) and conversely at 28 below παρορᾶν.
But even in authors of the classical period the distinction is
not always rigorously observed: e.g. Demosthenes oscillates

39

between σκοπεῖτε and σκέψασθε in what appear to be similar contexts.

21. εἰς διδασκάλου, with ellipse of οἰκίαν, is Attic idiom; cf. Plato, *Protagoras* 326c5. [The reading is probably correct, although found by Boulenger in only four MSS., including EH, to which may be added Laud gr. 90 (13th or 14th cent.); the others and Syr II read διδασκάλους, which is intelligible, but cannot be right unless one assumes the other reading to have been introduced into the text by a copyist bent on improving the idiom of the text; this possibility should not be ruled out of court, cf. P. Maas, *Kleine Schriften*, Munich 1973, 327–48, G. J. Toomer, *Gnomon* 35.1963.270, and cf. the readings already cited above at 10–11 and 20.]

24. ἥκω with a future participle seems to be a way of saying 'I am about to'. The only other occurrence I have been able to find is in Galen 9.869, ἥκομεν ἐροῦντες (the passages cited in LSJ are irrelevant). Perhaps the phrase was part of the lecturer's vocabulary during the Second Sophistic period. ἥκω cannot be taken literally here, as it would imply that B. had travelled in order to speak to an audience, which is difficult to reconcile with the fact that this essay is an address to members of his family.

25–6. τὰ πηδάλια τῆς διανοίας παραδόντας is a phrase borrowed from Plato, *Clitophon* 408b2.

27–8. This is the proposition that B. is chiefly concerned to argue: some elements in pagan literature can be exploited to good effect, others are to be avoided. The idea recurs in iv.50–1 and in Gregory of Nazianzus, *PG* 36.508: ὅσον χρήσιμον αὐτῶν καρπούμενοι πρός τε ζωὴν καὶ ἀπόλαυσιν, ὅσον ἐπικίνδυνον διαφεύγομεν.

29. ἔνθεν ἑλών is a Homeric expression, e.g. *Odyssey* 8.500, 'taking it up from this point'. It was also a favourite phrase with Atticists, cf. Longinus 34.4 with D. A. Russell's note *ad loc.*; Philostratus, *Vitae sophistarum* 529, 572; Heliodorus, *Aethiopica* 5.16.

Chapter II develops the theme that the goods of this world are insignificant in comparison with those of the next. The

Scriptures must be studied in order to appreciate the latter, but until one reaches the age at which it is possible to understand them fully it is a good idea to train oneself by the study of other books that are not utterly different in spirit from the Scriptures.

2–3. οὔτ᾽ . . . οὔτε: in classical Attic this pair of negatives would not have been written in a sentence already containing a negative; οὐδέν would be followed by οὐδέ, repeated if necessary.

3. The assonance of νομίζομεν and ὀνομάζομεν goes back to Gorgias' declamation on Helen, 9. It was a trick of style likely to appeal to Atticists. It is also found at Plutarch, *Moralia* 759e and *Crassus* 2.3, Heliodorus, *Aethiopica* 2.32.1.

συντέλειαν: 'end, completion, full realisation'; the word is used in this sense in Hellenistic and Christian writers.

4. ἄχρι: 'limited to', as at IV.37 and VI.6. LSJ cite this usage (but translate it wrongly) from Demosthenes 8.77 and 23.122.

4–10. This sentence is a topos that can be traced back to Plato, *Republic* 491c.

[4. οὐκοῦν οὐ H appears to be the correct reading, whereas all other MSS. have οὔκουν, which in Attic is not used without γε; cf. Denniston 422–4 and 439.]

[8. ἄξιον εἶναι is the reading of H here; it results in an inferior clausula. For the omission of εἶναι cf. Plato, *Republic* 578b2.]

8. ἀποβλέπομεν is usually constructed with πρός or εἰς, but cf. V.34.

[10. παρασκευήν: MS. Glasgow 407–8 has κατασκευήν.]

11. LSJ suggest that σθένος is not used in classical prose except in the phrase παντὶ σθένει, chiefly as a formula in treaties.

12. ἐκεῖνον: one would expect αὐτόν, since the pronoun has the same reference as τοῦτον.

13–14. ὅπῃ καὶ ὅπως is pleonastic. The expression is found in Aeschylus, *Prometheus* 875.

15. ὁρμήν: 'desire', practically 'intention'.

15–16. The nephews are evidently too young to understand

41

a discussion about eternal life. Their youth is again emphasised at 27–8.

ἢ καθ' ὑμᾶς: ἢ ὑμῶν would be more regular syntax, but B. has conflated two constructions, the latter being ἀκοῦσαι μεῖζόν ἐστιν ἢ καθ' ὑμᾶς.

16. γε μὴν: this grouping of particles recurs below at III.9, IV.2, and IX.94. It is common in Atticist writers (Schmid, index s.v., and 1.182); Xenophon is the only classical writer to use it extensively (Denniston 347).

17–19. τὴν . . . . εὐδαιμονίαν: the elevation of B.'s style at this point leads to an extremely artificial order of words.

[19. After μέρει H inserts τῷ μεγέθει, which makes the sentence unreasonably complex; the words are probably an explanatory gloss.]

22. καθ' ὅσον: ὅσον should probably be read; καθ' is either a mistake by B. or a scribal repetition of κατὰ in the preceding line.

[For ἀληθῶν H has ἀληθινῶν, which gives equally good sense and clausula.]

24. τοῖς πᾶσι: 'in all respects', a usage found at Thucydides 2.64.4.

τοσούτῳ is parallel to ὅσῳ, but the construction changes so that τοσοῦτον would have been strictly accurate.

26. ⟨οἱ⟩ ἱεροὶ λόγοι, '*the* sacred scriptures', might have been expected. The words were also used by pagans to describe their holy books; cf. A. D. Nock, *Conversion*, Oxford 1933, 31.

26. ἀπορρήτων: 'mysteries'; Lampe shows that Christian writers use the word of the spiritual meaning of the scriptures.

[27. After ἡμᾶς H and Syr II add δογμάτων, which is not necessary for the sense and looks like a gloss.]

27. ἐκπαιδεύοντες: this compound verb is rare, but Plato has it at *Crito* 45d1.

28. τοῦ βάθους τῆς διανοίας: 'the depth of their meaning', a metaphorical sense of βάθος: a rather similar meaning is found in Plato, *Theaetetus* 184a.

29. ἐν is here almost instrumental, 'by means of'; perhaps 'with the help of' is the simplest rendering.

30. τῷ τῆς ψυχῆς ὄμματι: the phrase is borrowed from Plato, *Republic* 533d2.

προγυμναζόμεθα: the technical term among ancient educational theorists for a preliminary training, often used in the context of rhetoric (προπαιδεύω is also found). Editors print the verb as an indicative, but it would be at least as good as a jussive subjunctive, -ώμεθα, which is the reading found in the Glasgow MS.

31. τακτικοῖς: 'military exercises'; LSJ do not give an exact parallel for this sense.

32. χειρονομίαις: presumably the manipulation of weights held in the hands. It was also part of training in a gymnasium, Plutarch *Moralia* 747b; Synesius *De somniis* 20.

ὀρχήσεσι can have a military sense, since Plato, *Cratylus* 406d12, speaks of ἡ ἐν τοῖς ὅπλοις ὄρχησις.

33. παιδείας: editors usually print παιδιᾶς which, if correct, means 'recreations', but in the context this is not the required sense, and παιδείας, 'training', the reading of the Glasgow MS., Vat. gr. 415, Laud gr. 90, and Syr I and II, should be accepted instead.

34ff. The idea of the struggle which men face can be traced in classical sources such as Plato, *Republic* 608b, as well as in the Pauline epistles (Hebrews 12.1, I Corinthians 9.25).

36. εἰς δύναμιν: normal Attic phraseology would be κατὰ δύναμιν.

37–9. Every source, including pagan literature, from which some benefit for the formation of the character can be derived, must be exploited. Gregory of Nazianzus groups pagan authors into the same four categories for this purpose, *PG* 37.1579, verses 33–7.

37. λογοποιοῖς: here 'historians'.

40. Dyers occur in one of Plato's arguments from analogy, *Republic* 429de. The word used there is βαφεύς, while δευσοποιός is an adjective, as it normally is elsewhere.

41. ἄνθος: 'colour' is a suitable translation here. (LSJ give 'purple', but the following clause shows that it cannot be a specific colour word.)

43. μέλλοι is the reading of all MSS., and the optative seems particularly inappropriate in view of the meaning of the clause, which contains no notion of the potential or uncertain.

But the analogy of IX.69 and Lucian, *Phalaris* 1.8, φέρειν δὲ ἀνάγκη . . . . εἰ μέλλοιμεν ἐπικρατήσειν and *Juppiter confutatus* 18, εἴ γε τὰ δίκαια ὁ Μίνως δικάζειν μέλλοι, (the latter brought to my attention by Mr. M. D. Reeve), suggests that this apparently incorrect use of the optative may be an affectation of Atticist writers, who could not handle forms of the verb that had long disappeared from the spoken language. (Mr. Reeve suggests to me that they could have been led astray by a faulty reading such as μέλλοι at Plato, *Republic* 460c6.) L. de Sinner emended to μέλλει; similarly in the first Lucian passage Madvig proposed μέλλομεν.

ἀνέκπλυτος is a word culled from Plato, *Timaeus* 26c3.

[43. After ἡμῖν H and Syr II add ἅπαντα τὸν χρόνον, which may be a scribe's attempt to amplify or improve the text.]

44. τοῖς ἔξω: i.e. 'pagan'. The similar expression at IV.1, τὰ ἔξωθεν μαθήματα, is also common. See A.-M. Malingrey, *Philosophia*, Paris 1961 (*Études et commentaires* 40), 212–13.

44–5. προτελεσθέντες: 'initiated'. LSJ imply that this word is not used in classical prose.

[45. ἐπακουσόμεθα: here again three MSS., E H and Glasgow 407–8, offer a jussive subjunctive, -ώμεθα, but the future in 47 is against it.]

46–7. The same simile is found not only in Plato, *Republic* 515e–516b, but also in Plutarch, *Moralia* 36e.

Chapter III justifies the notion of studying another culture by citing the examples of Moses and Daniel. 1–4 state that if pagan culture is in any way similar to Christian, knowledge of it will be of use, while if it is different, an appreciation of the contrast will be instructive. Analogous arguments are used today in justifying the study of ancient civilisations.

1–2 τοῖς λόγοις: i.e. Christian and pagan ideals.

2. ἄν is the second word in the clause; see on 1.1 above.

6–11. I have not been able to trace this analogy to a particular source. Much the same notion can be seen in Seneca, *Letters* 41.7.

[6. τῷ: the reading of Y is τό, equally good stylistically. It is found in MSS. Auct. T. 4.16 and Cambridge Dd. 4.16, which also replace βρύειν by a synonym, βρίθειν.]

8. περισειόμενα: LSJ cite only two instances of this word, *Iliad* 19.382 and 22.315, both applied to ἔθειραι.

[ψυχῇ: the Tiflis MS., Auct. T. 4.16 and Cambridge Dd. 4.16 all read ψυχῆς, which is more closely parallel to the first half of the analogy. The variant may be simply a correction by a pedantic scribe.]

προηγουμένως: 'principally', a technical term of philosophers, found from the time of Theophrastus onwards.

9. ἡ θύραθεν σοφία, like its synonym τὰ ἔξωθεν μαθήματα in IV.I, became a standard expression for pagan culture.

10. For the phraseology cf. Aristotle, *De plantis* 199a25 οἷον τὰ φύλλα τῆς τοῦ καρποῦ ἕνεκα σκέπης.

11. τοίνυν marks the transition from a general proposition to a particular instance; cf. Denniston 576. [Some MSS. have τοι, which is no improvement.]

12. For Moses and Egypt see Acts 7.22. It is worth noting in passing that Moses' wisdom had been cited by the earlier Jewish apologists Josephus and Philo as evidence of the superior antiquity of their culture to Greek; cf. H. Chadwick, *Early Christian thought and the classical tradition*, Oxford 1966, 13f. In turn Christian apologists claimed that Solon and Plato admired Moses' wisdom, e.g. Cyril of Alexandria, *PG* 76.525ab.

ὁ πάνυ: 'the great, the one and only', a common idiom in Atticist writers. The origin of the expression is obscure. It is allegedly found in Thucydides 8.1 and 8.89, but the former passage is not analogous and the latter is corrupt. At Xenophon, *Memorabilia* 3.5.1, apparently the only other instance, the words Περικλεῖ δέ ποτε τῷ τοῦ πάνυ Περικλέους διαλεγόμενος may imply the meaning 'great' or 'genuine', as was seen by J. Marshall in his edition (Oxford 1890), to which Mr. M. D. Reeve drew my attention.

15. τοῦ ὄντος: B. refers to reality in Platonic terms.

κάτω: 'later'. LSJ do not cite the use of this adverb in expressions of time from any author earlier than Plutarch.

16. For Daniel see the Book of Daniel 1.4–5.

[16–17 τὴν Χαλδαίων σοφίαν is phrased in exactly the same way as τοῖς Αἰγυπτίων μαθήμασιν. The change of word order and insertion of the definite article, as found in some MSS., τὴν σοφίαν (τῶν) Χαλδαίων, also result in acceptable Greek but are not improvements.]

Chapter IV discusses the elements in classical Greek literature, especially poetry, that will be beneficial or harmful to the young Christian.

1. ἄχρηστον: the neuter singular is used as if B. were going to continue with a subject such as ἡ παίδευσις. The sentence would then be one of a type common in Attic, especially in maxims or proverbs, e.g. Plato, *Republic* 354a οὐδέποτ' ἄρα λυσιτελέστερον ἀδικία δικαιοσύνης. Cf. KG 1.58–60.

3–4. τοῖς παρὰ τῶν ποιητῶν: 'the stories from the poets'.

[5. κατὰ τοὺς λόγους is omitted by several MSS. (Boulenger's DIYZ, the Tiflis MS., Auct. T. 4.16 and Cambridge Dd. 4.16). The phrase makes good sense but is not absolutely essential and could have been added to amplify the meaning. Syr I and II have it.]

5. ἐφεξῆς or ἑξῆς in conjunction with πᾶς means 'absolutely, without exception'. The expression recurs at VIII.2. It is common among the Atticists and derives from passages such as Thucydides 7.29.4 and Demosthenes 9.69 (see also D. A. Russell's edition of Longinus, Oxford 1964, xxv n.1).

προσέχειν: the syntax is difficult. One expects the infinitive to be governed by δεῖ, but B. postpones this verb to line 9. Toup (in MS. Clarendon Press d. 48 foll. 161ᵛ–2ᵛ) proposed to insert δεῖ. There is a sentence with a not quite identical difficulty below at VII.18–21, which might suggest that this syntactical oddity is a characteristic of B.'s usage. A remotely conceivable alternative is that B. intended the infinitive to be taken as an imperative, an Attic usage which would be possible in Atticist Greek, cf. Schmid 4.618.

[6. Boulenger suggested the deletion of τάς. If any change

46

is to be made here I should prefer to delete τὰς τῶν. But I cannot see anything wrong with the text.]

7. ἀγαπᾶν τε καὶ ζηλοῦν: cf. II.11 ἀγαπᾶν τε καὶ διώκειν.

9. μιμήσει: this term has its origin in Plato's discussion of poetry in the *Republic*. [ταῦτα: ταύτῃ is an error by assimilation of endings in MSS. CDEIY.]

ἐπιφρασσομένους: the earliest instance of this word cited by LSJ is Theophrastus, *Historia plantarum* 9.3.2. Notice that the Atticist writer does not adhere to the Attic spelling –ττ– for –σσ–.

10–11. For Odysseus and the Sirens cf. *Odyssey* 12.39ff., 154ff. Plutarch alludes to the episode in a similar context at *Moralia* 15d.

12. πράγματα: in the classical idiom ἔργα would have been written.

13. Cf. Proverbs 4.23 πάσῃ φυλακῇ τήρει σὴν καρδίαν.

[14. τι: MSS. ABC have τινα, which is a possible variant.]

15. δηλητήρια: 'poison'. For the use of the word in a similar context cf. Theophilus of Antioch, *Ad Autolycum* 2.12. The idea of honey on the lip of a cup to make medicine palatable was a well known topos, going back to Plato, *Laws* 659e.

16. The words ἐν πᾶσιν supplied by Desrousseaux are necessary for the sense of the passage. [Their loss is perhaps explained by the occurrence of some of the same letters in the following word, which caused a scribe's eye to jump ahead. Both Syriac versions correspond to the Greek manuscripts here.]

16ff. Embarrassing passages of Homer had led to the development of allegorical interpretation as early as Theagenes of Rhegion (*c*. 525 B.C.); on him see further R. Pfeiffer, *History of classical scholarship*, Oxford 1968, 9–11. They were a commonplace in the argument between pagans and Christians. The present passage seems to be directly dependent on Plato, *Republic* 377e–378e, 390ab, 395d, 396cd, where there are verbal similarities.

18. τραπέζῃ πληθούσῃ refers to the Phaeacians' luxury as described in the *Odyssey*, 9.5–10.

[21. H mistakenly has οὐδὲ τούτων.]

[23. γονεύς is the reading of most MSS. and Syr I: γονεῖς is found in Vat. gr. 415 and Syr II: Laud gr. 90, Auct. T. 4.16 and Cambridge Dd. 4.16 have γονεῦσι, which attaches the phrase to the following instead of the preceding clause.]

[26. Z, Auct. T. 4.16 and Cambridge Dd. 4.16 omit Διός. The word could be an intrusive gloss, but there is no positive reason for suspecting it, and Syr I and II also have it.]

27–8. Cf. A. H. M. Jones, *The Later Roman empire 284–602*, Oxford 1964, 1020: 'The drama had by the fourth century— and probably long before—given way to the mime, which was apparently a kind of ballet. . . . The actors or dancers, both male and female, though many of them were popular idols, were a despised class, very strongly reprobated by Christian sentiment and excluded from membership of the church unless they left the stage.' For another comment on the stage see VI.17.

29. ψυχαγωγίας: the technical term for the persuasive effect of stylistic grace or charm, found e.g. in Plato, *Phaedrus* 261a8 (used there of rhetoric).

30. This idea about rhetoric may go back to a neighbour-ing passage of the *Phaedrus*, 259e7–260a4.

καὶ . . . . δὲ: Denniston 199 says 'this is a natural enough combination, the former particle denoting that something is added, the latter that what is added is distinct from what precedes'. It is fairly common in Attic prose and in Lucian (*ibid.* 201). [Toup's emendation καὶ . . . . δὴ is unnecessary.]

34. Avoidance of litigation was not merely a Christian principle, e.g. I Corinthians 6.1–7, but the Stoics also recommended it, Musonius 54.7.

34ff. The idea seems to be paraphrased in Gregory of Nazianzus' poem, *PG* 37.1580, lines 36–44.

36ff. The simile of the bee is a common topos in ancient writing. The present passage bears a close resemblance to Plutarch, *Moralia* 79cd.

36. ἀνθέων: this uncontracted form instead of ἀνθῶν is found in Attic verse, Xenophon and Koine Greek. [The MSS. here are about equally divided between the two.]

37. ἄχρι: see on II.4 above.

[42. ἡμῖν, the reading of DHIX Syr I, accords with the verbs in 46 and 48 better than ὑμῖν, the reading of other MSS. and Syr II.]

44. οὔτε μὴν: Denniston 341 cites four examples of this uncommon grouping of particles from Xenophon.

ἐπιπτῶσιν: LSJ suggest that the active form of the aorist of this verb is post-classical.

46. ἀφῆκαν: instead of this gnomic aorist one expects the standard Attic idiom ἐῶσιν, 'dismiss from their minds'.

48ff. The rose and its thorns may have been another common topos; however, the parallel passage cited by commentators, Lucian *De historia conscribenda* 28, is not very similar.

49. ῥοδωνιᾶς: 'rose-bush', as used by Theophrastus in his botanical books. Atticists sometimes use this word in preference to ῥόδον; for the sake of emphasis the longer word replaces the shorter (cf. Latin *quo is?* and *quo vadis?*).

τοῦ ἄνθους appears to be a partitive genitive dependent on δρεψάμενοι, a highly unclassical construction which can be paralleled in Philostratus, *Heroicus* 663. [S. Witkowski, *Gnomon* 12.1936.356, proposed to read δρεψόμενοι, an improvement more specious than real: the aorist can be justified by the fact that after picking a rose one still tries to avoid the thorns on the stem.]

[50–1. In place of ὅσον χρήσιμον καρπωσάμενοι H has τὸ ἡδὺ λαβόντες, which is probably a copyist's simplification of the text. It receives no support from Syr I and II.]

[51. φυλαξώμεθα: the jussive subjunctive is the reading of most MSS., including Vat. gr. 415 and Glasgow 407–8. A few MSS. have the future, parallel to the verb in 48, and some editors adopt this.]

52. προσῆκε is used here and at VII.35, IX.72, X.9 below as if it were προσήκει. The justification of the usage is hard to see. B. may have been influenced by two examples in Xenophon, *Anabasis* 7.7.18 and *De re equestri* 12.14, where the MSS. have the imperfect and editors frequently restore the present. [It is doubtful whether we should place any trust in the late Byzantine lexicographer Thomas Magister, who says (p. 287

Ritschl) τὸ δὲ προσῆκεν ἀντὶ τοῦ προσήκει λαμβανόμενον Ἀττικόν ἐστιν, ὥσπερ καὶ τὸ ἔδει ἀντὶ τοῦ δεῖ.]

53–4. The Doric proverb is given by Leutsch-Schneidewin, *Paroemiographi graeci* II p. 775. While it is cited by the fathers I have not found any use of it in a classical author that is likely to have served as B.'s source.

Chapter V gives examples of useful lessons to be derived from pagan writers, especially poets. Homer, Hesiod, Theognis and Prodikos are cited.

1–2. There is some doubt about the text. The MSS. read καθεῖναι δεῖ τὸν ἡμέτερον. If καθεῖναι is right we perhaps have an instance of the intransitive use of this verb, known both in classical and later Greek, followed here by ἐπί instead of εἰς, e.g. καθιέναι εἰς ἀγῶνα, 'to enter a struggle, competition', as in Plutarch *Moralia* 616d and Lucian *Alexander* 6. [Toup proposed the present infinitive καθιέναι, but we have already seen at 1.28 that B. is not rigorous in his observation of aspects.]

More drastic emendations have been tried. Since ἡμῖν and ἡμέτερον may be thought repetitive, Ragon proposed ἕτερον, referring to life in the next world as at II.9. This reading is not fully satisfactory in conjunction with καθεῖναι, and Desrousseaux proposed καταθεῖναι, 'to build up a treasure', which LSJ do not cite except in the middle voice and with an expressed object. A better way of dealing with the repetition of the personal pronoun may be to read ὑμῖν, which is implied by Syr II.

1. ἡμῖν: the dative with δεῖ instead of the accusative is extremely rare. The best attested classical example is Euripides, *Hippolytus* 940; a less certain case is Xenophon, *Memorabilia* 3.3.10, where Stobaeus quotes the text with an accusative. The alternative construction was no doubt made possible by the analogy with προσήκει. [MSS. Glasgow 407–8 and Vat. gr. 415 place ἡμῖν after ἀρετῆς, which may be right, so as to separate it more widely from ἡμέτερον.]

5–6. The receptivity of young minds to ethical lessons is

emphasised by Seneca, *Letters* 108.12 and Plutarch, *Moralia* 3ef.

7. ἀμετάστατα: both the word and the notion are taken from Plato, *Republic* 378e.

9. The verses of Hesiod are *Works and Days* 286–92, which should be compared with Matthew 7.13–14. The Hesiod passage was often quoted in antiquity; B. presumably derived his knowledge of it from Plato, *Republic* 364cd, because he also borrows from the same passage the words τραχεῖα and ἀνάντης.

10. ᾄδουσιν means no more than 'say' or perhaps 'repeat'. The usage is common in Atticistic Greek and the semantic change is specifically attested by Strabo 1.2.6.

οὐχὶ is pleonastic; it appears to result from the confusion of two possible constructions, ἢ προτρέπειν / εἰ μὴ προτρέποντα.

προτρέποντα: 'encouraging', especially to the study of philosophy, hence the technical term λόγος προτρεπτικός, as in 19 below. The occurrence of the word here hints at the category of literature which the present essay belongs to, as was seen by Norden (cited on 31 below), and M. Pohlenz.

[13. The omission of ὁδός by HZ is simply a blunder.]

14. προσβῆναι: the context suggests the relatively rare meaning 'climb'. [προσβάντα ABX and Glasgow 407–8: προσβάντι the other MSS. There is nothing to choose between the two, but perhaps the accusative was assimilated to the surrounding datives in the majority of MSS.] [διὰ in H is a blunder caused by the occurrence of the word earlier in the line.]

15. ὄρθιον: the steepness of the hill was proverbial, and Lucian, *Vera historia* 2.18, exploits it for a joke against the Stoics (τῶν δὲ Στωικῶν οὐδεὶς παρῆν· ἔτι γὰρ ἐλέγοντο ἀναβαίνειν τὸν τῆς ἀρετῆς ὄρθιον λόφον).

17. ἀθρόον refers to κακίαν. The adjective was sometimes two-termination in Attic, e.g. Demosthenes 19.228. [There is no need to follow the MSS. CEZ by restoring ἀθρόαν.] B. is paraphrasing the word ἰλαδὸν in verse 287 of Hesiod and says 'which exists in quantity, close at hand for the taking, as this same poet said'.

[19. προτρέπων: H gives the middle form προτρεπόμενος which is equally good.]

21. ὥστε: B. writes a consecutive clause instead of a final

clause. KG 2.504 show that there are precedents for this in Xenophon.

[24. Many MSS. have the slight orthographical error of writing an indicative instead of the jussive subjunctive.]

25. τινος may refer to the famous rhetorician and writer Libanios, whose acquaintance B. had probably made in Constantinople during the years around 350 (P. Maas, *SB* Berlin 1912.1117–18; G. Bardy, *Dictionnaire d'histoire et géographie ecclésiastique*, s.v. Basile, column 1112).

26–7. This view of Homer's poetry, which helped it to maintain its position in the educational curriculum, is seen in Dio Chrysostom 43, Horace *Epistles* 1.2.1–4 and most fully in the scholia on the *Iliad* which are known by the name 'exegetical' (designated as such in the new edition by H. Erbse, Berlin 1969– , in progress). In these scholia the attempt to draw a moral lesson from each episode is taken to great lengths; for some amusing examples see the scholia on *Iliad* 1.193–4, 490–1, 512, 520, 523, 566, 611.

[26. CH omit ἤ, which may be right.]

27–8. ὅ τι μὴ πάρεργον is a rather glib way of dismissing those episodes in Homer which had made allegorical interpretation fashionable.

28–46 deal with a famous episode from *Odyssey* 6.135ff. It was used to point a different moral, namely that the resourceful man can achieve surprising successes even when destitute, by Musonius 46.3 and Epictetus 3.26.33. It is also referred to by Libanios, *Encomium of Odysseus* 21 (ed. Foerster 8.233–4): ἧς (the island of the Phaeacians) καὶ γυμνὸς ἐπιβὰς ἐθαυμάζετο παραχρῆμα μὲν ὑπὸ τῆς Ἀλκινόου θυγατρός, μικρὸν δ' ὕστερον πεῖραν αὑτοῦ διδοὺς ὑφ' ἁπάντων.

29. πεποίηκε: 'has portrayed', a common usage in classical prose.

30. αἰδέσαι: 'inspired respect'. The active forms of this verb are not attested earlier than the fourth century A.D.

φανέντα μόνον: i.e. before he had time to explain his identity. In fact, according to Homer, Nausicaa stood her ground because of the strength given to her by Athena, and Odysseus, after a moment's thought, decided to speak to her. B. alters the story slightly to suit his purpose, and we do not need to consider seriously E. Norden's drastic and arbitrary supplement φανέντα μόνον <ἔπειτα δὲ διαλεχθέντα πολλῷ μᾶλλον καταιδέσαι αὐτήν>, *Jahrbücher für klassische Philologie*, Supplementband 19, 1892. 383 note 3.

31. τοσούτου δεῖν: 'far from'. For the history of this type of construction see J. Wackernagel, *Vermischte Beiträge zur griechischen Sprachkunde* = *Kleine Schriften*, Göttingen 1956, 1.779ff. Originally the infinitive was 'limitative' and appeared only in the expressions ὀλίγου δεῖν, μικροῦ δεῖν; then it was extended to πολλοῦ δεῖν as in Demosthenes 23.7.

ὀφλῆσαι: the classical form was ὀφλεῖν, unless one accepts the MS. reading ὤφλησε at Lysias 13.65.

32. ἀρετῇ ἀντὶ ἱματίων: the phrase is found in Plato, *Republic* 457a5–6, in a dissimilar context. John Chrysostom, *PG* 47.338, has οὐδὲ γυμνὸν δεῖξαι δυνήσῃ ἕως ἂν τὰ τῆς ἀρετῆς ἱμάτια περικείμενος ᾖ.

[33–4. For ἄξιον νομισθῆναι H has ἀξίαν νομισθῆναι τὴν ἀρετήν, which upsets the balance of the period and may have been partly inspired by ἀρετῇ in the previous line.]

[34. EH Syr II read εἰς ἐκεῖνον, but cf. 11.8 above.]

36. εἶναι is pleonastic as at x.3 below. Cf. KG 2.29.

40. συνεκνήχεται: LSJ do not cite the word, but give the synonym συνεκκολυμβήσει in some other formulations of the idea, e.g. the one ascribed to Aristippus by Galen, *Protreptikos* 5 (p. 108. 18 Marquardt); for a collection of the material see Favorinus fr.117 (ed. Barigazzi, Florence 1966).

44. The analogy with dice can be traced back to Plato, *Republic* 604c6.

45. ἀναφαίρετον: 'inalienable': the idea is ascribed to the Cynic Antisthenes by Diogenes Laertius 6.12.

48–50. Solon 15.2–4. The lines are also found as Theognis 316–18, and are quoted by Plutarch, *Moralia* 78c, 92e, 472d.

53–4: Theognis 157–8. In 54 δὲ destroys the metre, but late Greek writers tend to insert this particle into poetic quotations where the syntactical structure permits. [ἄλλως is also the reading given in Stobaeus 4.32.36, whereas the MSS. of Theognis have ἄλλῳ.]

55–77 refer to a famous work of the sophist Prodikos of Ceos, which contained the allegory of Herakles standing at the fork in the road. Prodikos' own work seems to have been lost even in antiquity but it is very frequently referred to, and our chief source of information is Xenophon, *Memorabilia* 2.1.21–34. Thanks to Xenophon and B. the allegory enjoyed a great vogue in the Renaissance and was taken as a subject by many painters: see E. Panofsky, *Herkules am Scheideweg*, Leipzig 1930.

55. που . . . . τῶν ἑαυτοῦ συγγραμμάτων: 'somewhere in his writings'. The usage of που is in accordance with classical Attic, but the phrase is very laboured when contrasted with Xenophon's ἐν τῷ ξυγγράμματι, especially considering that B. could not read this or any other of Prodikos' works in the original text.

After the word σοφιστής the MSS. EH and Laud gr. 90 add the name Πρόδικος. This is presumably no more than an explanatory gloss. Neither Syriac version has it. It is notable that B.'s nephews are of an age and/or a precocity to know who the Cean sophist was.

58. ἀπόβλητος is rare in classical prose but common in the Atticists.

58–9. οὕτω πως . . . . μέμνημαι: B. follows Xenophon's wording ὧδέ πως λέγων, ὅσα ἐγὼ μέμνημαι.

61. Herakles is stated to be very young, whereas in Xenophon the wording is ἐκ παίδων εἰς ἥβην ὡρμᾶτο, which might suggest an age of about fifteen or sixteen. It is uncertain whether we should infer that this was the age of B.'s nephews.

κομιδῇ: in normal Attic prose this word would be next to the adjective it qualifies. Schmid gives no example from the Atticists of the word order seen here in the text.

62. ἄγοντι: ἔχοντι would be expected.

63. Xenophon has the very similar wording ποτέραν τῶν ὁδῶν τράπηται.

68. διαρρεῖν: 'to be dissolute'; LSJ cite this usage from Plutarch and Lucian.

69. ἐσμόν: for the metaphorical use of the word see Plato, *Republic* 450b1 ἐσμὸς λόγων: at 574d2 he has ἡδονῶν σμῆνος.

ἐξηρτημένην: the passive is used as if it were middle, in the sense of 'having something hung on oneself' (LSJ cite examples from classical authors).

[ἐξηρτημένον, as in MS. Vat. gr. 415, is unnecessary.]

71. κατεσκληκέναι: the idea that Virtue is withered and of unattractive appearance is an important modification of the story as found in Xenophon and indicates an adaptation to suit Cynic ideals. The word used here is not cited by LSJ from Attic prose earlier than Theophrastus.

76. θεὸν γενέσθαι: it is remarkable that a Christian father should make no other comment on this phrase than ὡς ὁ ἐκείνου λόγος. The expression in Xenophon is less explicit, but B. was no doubt familiar with Plato, *Theaetetus* 176b1, ὁμοίωσις θεῷ.

Chapter VI warns against the danger of allowing one's conduct to fall short of the principles one expresses publicly. B.'s treatment of the theme is superficial; he does not tackle the famous problem, discussed by Aristotle, of the man who knows that an action is contrary to one of his moral principles but nevertheless performs it.

1. καί, though presumably intended to emphasise λόγος, seems otiose.

λόγος: 'reputation', not found in Attic prose in this sense according to LSJ.

2. μεῖζον: adverbial. LSJ cite only the dubious parallel of Demosthenes, *Letters* 3.28, where a payrus offers the variant μᾶλλον.

εἰς: κατά might be expected in this phrase.

3. ἑαυτῶν is unnecessary for the sense and would not have been written by an Attic author. [MS. Laud gr. 90 omits it.]

[There is little to choose between πειστέον, the reading of most MSS., and πιστευτέον (ABCX and Glasgow 407–8), which is supported by VII.16.]

4. δεικνύναι: 'make a reality of', rather an extension of the Attic meaning.

55

7. The quotation is *Odyssey* 10.495, about Teiresias; it is cited by Plato, *Republic* 386d7 and *Meno* 100a5.

9. θαυμαστόν τι οἶον κάλλος is almost exactly repeated at VII.41. The idea is reminiscent of Plato, *Republic* 472d4–5 ζωγράφον ὃς ἂν γράψας παράδειγμα οἶον εἴη ὁ κάλλιστος ἄνθρωπος.

[10. H has αὐτός τις. If τις were right the natural word order would be τοιοῦτός τις. Probably it is intrusive, resulting from τι in the previous line.]

[12. ἐπαινέσαι: H has ἐπαινεῖν, which is strictly parallel to ἀποτείνειν and may be right; but cf. on I.20 and 28.]

13. ἀποτείνειν is a favourite word with Plato, cf. *Gorgias* 458b7, *Republic* 605d1, *Protagoras* 336c6.

15–18. The contrast between the social station of actors and the parts they played on the stage was a commonplace among moralists, e.g. Seneca, *Letters* 80.7–8. Legal texts make it clear that some actors were slaves, e.g. Gaius 3.212, Ulpian in *Digest* 21.1.38.14 and 32.73.3. See J. E. Spruit, *De juridische en sociale positie der romeinse acteurs*, Assen 1966.

[16. The reading βασιλέας πολλάκις καὶ δυνάστας of ABHX is a strange aberration.]

17. οὐδὲ μὲν οὖν: 'nor indeed'; in classical Greek μέν would have been omitted.

18. The analogy of the λύρα and χορός is drawn from Plato, *Gorgias* 482bc. There is no need to look further afield in such sources as Diogenes Laertius 6.27.

21. αὐτὸς δέ τις ἕκαστος κτλ: 'is each individual to be in conflict with himself?'. αὐτός τις ἕκαστος is a phrase also found in B.'s contemporary Heliodorus 7.5. Although ἕκαστός τις is an Attic idiom, it is not certain that B.'s word order would have seemed correct to an Athenian.

22–4. The quotation, in which the metre is broken by the intrusion of a particle as at v.54, is the notorious line of Euripides, *Hippolytos* 612. Although Hippolytos did not break his oath, the line was mercilessly attacked by Aristophanes, *Thesmophoriazusae* 275 and *Frogs* 101, 1471. The quotations in Plato, *Symposium* 199a and *Theaetetus* 154d do not give the complete line.

24. Cf. Aeschylus, *Seven against Thebes* 592, οὐ γὰρ δοκεῖν

ἄριστος ἀλλ' εἶναι θέλει, cited by (among others) Plato, *Republic* 361b.

26. The passage of Plato referred to is *Republic* 361a.

Chapter VII is a series of anecdotes about famous pagan personalities which illustrate various Christian moral principles.

2. οὕτως: 'without more ado'.

[ἀποδεχώμεθα: the jussive subjunctive is the reading of HZ, Auct. T. 4.16, Cambridge Dd. 4.16 and Glasgow 407–8, and fits in well with 5 below and v.24. Other MSS. have the indicative.]

[ἐπειδή EH: ἐπεί other MSS. The former is more likely in Attic, but there is no certainty that B. wrote it.]

3. ἀκολουθίᾳ: 'sequence', 'tradition'; Hellenistic in this sense.

πρὸς ἡμᾶς: 'up to our own time'; not an Attic usage, if LSJ can be trusted, but πρὸς ἑσπέραν is found, so the extension of usage is very slight.

5–11. This story is found in Plutarch, *Pericles* 5, but with the difference that Pericles sent a slave to accompany the man home and did not go himself. Gregory of Nazianzus, *PG* 37.833a, tells the same story in iambic verse.

[7. διήρκεσαν FHU: διήρκεσε other MSS. and Syr I and II.]

8–9. ὁ δὲ . . . αὐτῷ: τῷ δὲ οὐ μέλον would be better syntax. B. shows off his knowledge of the accusative absolute and creates anacolouthon.

11–14. The anecdote about Euclides the Socratic can be found in Plutarch, *Moralia* 462c and 489d, Stobaeus 4. p.659, 662 Hense; see also L. Sternbach, *Gnomologium Vaticanum* 278 (reprinted Berlin 1963, p.108). The story is also told of Socrates.

[13. ἱλεώσεσθαι Boulenger's *recentiores* and Auct. T. 4.16, Cambridge Dd. 4.16: most others have ἱλεώσασθαι, but the aorist infinitive after a verb of swearing with future intention is not very well attested; KG 1.197.]

16–18. An inaccurate quotation of Euripides, *Rhesus* 84 ἁπλοῦς ἐπ᾽ ἐχθροῖς μῦθος ὁπλίζειν χέρα.

[17. λεγούσῃ ἁπλῶς H.]

[18. The MSS. have χέρα or χεῖρα; there is no certainty that B. retained the correct metrical form.]

19. χαλινόν: a common metaphor in classical poetry, cf. LSJ, and found in Plato, *Phaedrus* 246a.

18–21. It seems necessary to supply the main verb δεῖ, understood as implied by πιστευτέον. Cf. above on IV.5.

23–30. This anecdote is found in Gregory of Nazianzus, *PG* 35.596 and, in a more intelligible form, at Diogenes Laertius 6.33 and 6.89. The subject of the story is different in each case.

29. ἐπιγράψαι: this impossible feat is absent from the accounts in Diogenes, which show that the victim wrote on a slip of papyrus and then stuck that on his forehead.

29–30. τὸν δημιουργόν: B.'s grasp of syntax deserts him unexpectedly: ὁ δημιουργός would be normal.

[30. Some MSS. have τοσούτον, an erroneous anticipation of 35.]

31–2. This explicit statement is an important indication of B.'s views.

34–8. Cf. St. Matthew 5.39, 5.44.

34. κατά with a genitive after verbs of striking has an Attic parallel in κατὰ κόρρης, Demosthenes 19.197 (the Gospel has ἐπί here).

35–6. τὸ . . . Εὐκλείδου: ἀδελφόν is to be supplied from 33.

38–40. Another important statement of principle: if one is first made acquainted with these examples from pagan antiquity, one will realise that Christian precepts can be realised in one's own life. No one who regretted the position that the pagan authors held in the school curriculum would have expressed himself in these terms.

38. προπαιδευθείς: the concept of preparatory training goes back ultimately to Plato, *Republic* 536d.

40. διαπιστήσειεν: the compound verb is rare, although found in Demosthenes 19.324; perhaps it was chosen to make a good clausula.

[οὐδ' Desrousseaux: the MSS. have οὐκ, but a connecting word is required.]

40–4. The story about Alexander is found in Arrian 4.19.6, Plutarch, *Life of Alexander* 21 and *Moralia* 338de, but in all those instances it is the wife of Darius, not his daughters, who is mentioned.

[42. παρέχειν: DH have ἔχειν, which may be no more than a scribal attempt to simplify the text.]

μαρτυρουμένας: 'reported', 'well known for'; this passive usage of the verb is Hellenistic according to LSJ.

[43. τὸν ἄνδρας ἑλόντα AX: τοὺς ἄνδρας ἑλόντα H: τοὺς ἄνδρας ἑλόντας most other MSS. and Syr I and II.]

44–7. Cf. St. Matthew 5.28.

47–53. The anecdote about Cleinias is found, without mention of his name, in Iamblichus, *Life of Pythagoras* 144. B. appears to make the remarkable statement that Cleinias was inspired by Christian precepts. It is by no means inconceivable that B. read Iamblichus, since the *Life of Pythagoras* seems to have been known to Athanasios when writing his *Life of St. Antony*: see R. Reitzenstein, *SB* Heidelberg 1914.8.14–18, 30–3, 38–9, 59 (I owe this reference to the Revd. A. Meredith).

51. ὁ δέ is pleonastic; it would have been correct if the sentence began ἐξῆν μέν.

[52–3. δοκεῖν is acceptable; cf. KG 2.19; some MSS. have δοκεῖ.]

53. Cf. St. Matthew 5.34ff.

In Chapter VIII B. turns from educational practice to more general considerations about the purpose of an individual's existence.

1–3. Cf. 1.27 above.

[2. ἐφεξῆς DHI: ἑξῆς other MSS.; cf. IV.5.]

[4. ἅ MSS.: εἰ Desrousseaux, which is possible.]

5. 'carrying all before us like a torrent'. παρασύρω is used often of rivers, e.g. Aristophanes, *Knights* 527 and Longinus

32.4. A partial analogy occurs in Plutarch, *Moralia* 5f, πόλεμος χειμάρρου δίκην πάντα σύρων καὶ πάντα παραφέρων (imitated by Anna Comnena in the preface to her history). [The MSS. are divided between χειμάρρουν παρασύροντας and χειμάρρου παρασύροντος.]

6. ἐμβάλλεσθαι: 'to take on board', a Hellenistic usage.

7–12. The argument by analogy from crafts is obviously Platonic in inspiration, even if the parallel of Plato, *Republic* 488cd, cited by the editors, is not very exact.

8–9. κατὰ σκοποῦ: LSJ imply that this usage is post-classical and cite the historian Herodian 6.7.8.

9. καὶ μὲν δὴ καὶ: cf. Denniston 395–7.

9–10. Xenophon, *Memorabilia* 1.1.7, uses χαλκευτικός and τεκτονικός together, but the context is not otherwise similar.

10. τοῦ . . . . τέλους: a more natural and simple expression would have been τοῦ τῆς τέχνης τέλους; cf. 1.8–9 above.

11. γε: 'that is', explanatory: Denniston 138–9.

12–14. οὐ γὰρ δὴ . . . οὐκ: 'it is not the case that X . . ., while Y . . .', a classical construction well imitated.

12. χειρωνακτῶν: classical Attic used δημιουργός instead of this Ionic word.

13. πέρας: 'object', post-classical in this sense.

15. τοῖς ἀλόγοις: 'animals', as at Plato, *Protagoras* 321b8. [Several MSS. and Syr I omit παντάπασι.]

16–18. Ships without ballast are a metaphor in Plato, *Theaetetus* 144a, and the rudder is part of a similar metaphor at Aeschylus, *Agamemnon* 802.

19. ὥσπερ: the construction is not completed by οὕτως, a fact which complicates the other problems in the sentence.

[20. τοῖς μουσικῆς was proposed by De Sinner, whereas nearly all the MSS. have τῆς μουσικῆς, and a few have τοῖς μουσικοῖς. μουσικὸς ἀγών is a phrase attested in Aristophanes, *Plutus* 1164; Plato, *Laws* 658a, 828c; Plutarch, *Life of Pericles* 13. On the other hand Pollux 3.142 says that Attic authors οὐ ῥᾳδίως λέγουσιν ἀγῶνας μουσικούς, ἀλλὰ μουσικῆς. Did B. follow him?]

20–2. The meaning of this obscurely phrased sentence should be: 'one must practise for the particular contest that one is about to enter.' The first clause can perhaps be translated 'training is undertaken for those competitions in which there are prizes (announced)'. MSS. EH and Laud gr. 90 add πρόκεινται, which makes the sense clearer, but may be an interpolation of scribes with that intention. Syr I and II offer nothing more than a confused paraphrase. The chief difficulty is μελετᾷ in 22, which needs to mean 'enter' or 'perform'. I have found no parallel and wonder if the word is a corruption arising from μελέται in 20.

22–4. Pausanias 6.5.6 records Polydamas' feat of strength. Plato, *Republic* 338c, cited by previous editors, does not seem to be B.'s source.

22. οὔκουν . . . . ἀλλ᾽: 'at least Polydamas did not, instead he . . . .' For the particles see Denniston 423.

24–7. Milo's exploit is recorded in Pausanias 6.14.6, with the difference that there a discus is mentioned.

27. μολύβδῳ συνδεδεμένοι: lead was used as an adhesive between the base of a statue and its plinth.

ἀπαξαπλῶς: the word is post-classical.

28–9. 'But if they had meddled with . . . .'. περιειργάσαντο would be more normal; perhaps B. intended the imperfect to be taken as conative.

Marsyas and Olympos were Phrygians, believed to be the inventors of various kinds of music. They are mentioned in Plato, *Symposium* 215bc and in many other authors, e.g. Plutarch, *Moralia* 1133de and Dio Chrysostom, *De regno* 1.1.

30. ταχύ must be taken as ironical.

31. μὴ is pleonastic after διαφεύγω: see KG 2.208.

32. ἀλλὰ (. . . .) μέντοι is rare, but found in Plato and Xenophon; cf. Denniston 410.

32ff. Timotheos, the player of the oboe, is to be distinguished from his more famous namesake whose instrument was the κιθάρα.

34–5. τοσοῦτον αὐτῷ περιῆν, 'he was so superior in', is an idiom found already in Demosthenes 21.17.

36. καὶ μέντοι καὶ is another grouping of particles found especially in Xenophon and Plato; cf. Denniston 413.

[37. H has ἐκμαλάττειν.]

38–41. The anecdote is told in similar terms by Dio Chrysostom, *De regno* 1.1. Plutarch, *Moralia* 335a tells it to the credit of one Antigenidas, not Timotheos.

38. τὸ Φρύγιον ἐπαυλήσαντα: the Phrygian melody was evidently believed to encourage aggressive action, cf. Aristotle, *Politics* 1342b7; Plato, *Republic* 399a, disagreed. For more about the ancients' view of the power of music see below on IX.39.

The rare verb ἐπαυλεῖν was not used in classical Greek with the meaning 'play a melody'.

[41. τε: H has τῇ.]

46. συναυξήσαντες: if the preposition in this compound has any force it gives the meaning 'increased their strength along with the size of their bodies'.

[46. καὶ πολλὰ DH.]

46–7. ἐνιδρώσαντες: the verb is cited by LSJ only from Xenophon, *Symposium* 2.18.

52. The paltry nature of prizes at Greek athletic events has often been commented on, e.g. by St. Paul in I Corinthians 9.25. It seems, however, that the crowns of wild-olive and celery were replaced in the Hellenistic age by monetary prizes at some festivals. See H. A. Harris, *Sport in Greece and Rome*, London 1972, 26, 34, 41–2. The present passage raises the question whether the games still took place at the end of the fourth century, and Harris 42 cites evidence for the continuation of the Olympic games until A.D. 396 (Cedrenus 326d), the games at Antioch until A.D. 520 (Malalas 417.5). I have not been able to discover what happened in Cappadocia at this date.

56–7. ἐπ' ἄμφω καθεύδειν (τὰ ὦτα) was a well known proverb; Leutsch-Schneidewin, *Paroemiographi graeci* 1.409, appendix proverbiorum II.78.

59. Sardanapalos, king of Assyria, is first mentioned in Greek by Herodotus 2.150 and Aristophanes, *Birds* 1021. He is portrayed as the prime example of the hedonistic or effeminate life in Ctesias, fr.15, which is not much later in date, and soon became proverbial (Leutsch-Schneidewin, *Paroemiographi graeci* 1.449, 2.600).

59–60. τὰ πρῶτα . . . . ἐφέρετο: if τὰ πρῶτα is practically equivalent to πρῶτος, as at Herodotus 6.100, 9.78 and Aristophanes, *Frogs* 421, 'he would be considered first'; but one might also consider translating 'he would win the first rank'.

60. Margites, the proverbial simpleton of antiquity, was the subject of a lost poem ascribed by some to Homer. (The surviving frr. are edited by M. L. West, *Iambi et elegi graeci*, ii, Oxford 1972, 69–76.)

62. ἐπιτήδειον, as read by almost all the MSS. and Syr I, gives the meaning 'capable in any other of the things that are useful in life'. Boulenger adopted from MS. Paris. gr. 488 ἐπιτηδείων, 'any other of the useful occupations in life', which is not superior in sense. [It is found in Syr II.]

62–3. εἰ δὴ 'Ομήρου ταῦτα: this expression of scepticism is a hint that B. may be drawing on Clement of Alexandria's *Stromateis* 1.25.1 (2 p.16 Stählin) as his source here, since Clement expresses the same point with the words εἰ δὴ αὐτοῦ.

63. μή: 'perhaps', an Attic usage found at e.g. Plato, *Gorgias* 462e6.

Pittakos was one of the Seven Sages. His saying was criticised in detail by Plato, *Protagoras* 340c, which is doubtless B.'s source.

67. δὴ οὖν is a very rare collocation of particles except in Herodotus and Plato. It recurs in ix.3.

69. μέλλοιμεν: the optative weakens the force of the assertion which needs instead to be strengthened, 'unless indeed we are to incur . . . .'. Cf. ii.43 above.

72–3. τοῖς . . . . δικαιωτηρίοις: the separation of article and noun is an extreme example of hyperbaton. The noun is very rare; B. appears to be borrowing it from Plato, *Phaedrus* 249a6 τὰ ὑπὸ γῆς δικαιωτήρια.

76. παραίτησις: 'means of escape', literally 'intercession', 'means of begging off'. LSJ cite examples from classical Greek.

μὴ οὐχί: the negatives are pleonastic, but not unknown in Attic. Plato, *Gorgias* 461c2 has ἀπαρνήσεσθαι μὴ οὐχί; cf. Dodds' note on that passage, KG 2.210.

In Chapter IX the moralising tone continues, and in the opening part of it there is little reference to pagan culture.

2–3. σχολὴν ἀπό τινος ἄγειν 'to keep clear of', is an idiom cited by LSJ from Xenophon, *Cyropaedia* 8.3.47.

3–4. ὅτι μὴ πᾶσα ἀνάγκη: 'except under absolute compulsion'; the expression is borrowed verbatim from Plato, *Phaedo* 67a4.

5. The notion of the body as a prison of the soul is well known from Plato, e.g. *Phaedo* 62b, 67ad, 82d. and recurs later in this chapter (76ff.), where it is ascribed to Pythagoras. [τὰ τοῦ σώματος πάθη is the reading of most MSS., but the complexity of the expression and the repetition of τῶν παθῶν in 6–7 make it likely that we should adopt the reading τὸ σῶμα, found in AH, Vat. gr. 415 and Syr I and II.]

6. φιλοσοφίας: cf. on II.44.

7–8. For ὑπηρετεῖν with a direct object cf. Plato *Republic* 467a1 ὑπηρετεῖν τὰ περὶ τὸν πόλεμον, originally an accusative of respect. [ἥδιστα προσῆκεν BCH, which is quite wrong.]

8–9. τραπεζοποιούς: 'slaves who set out the tables'; a rare word, but I have not been able to discover whether B. borrowed it from a particular context.

9. περινοοῦντες: 'devoting their thoughts to', rare in classical Greek and not used in quite this sense.

9–10. The world-wide search for gastronomic delicacies was a favourite theme for moralists in the Roman empire. Cf. e.g. Musonius 103.13 and Philo, *De agricultura* 2.99–100 (Cohn-Wendland).

13–14. Three proverbial expressions describing the punishments of the damned in Hades (cf. Leutsch-Schneidewin, *Paroemiographi graeci* 1.130, 2.481.20, 1.343). [14. Some MSS. and Syr I have the clearly inferior variant τετριμμένον.]

16. This aphorism of Diogenes the Cynic is recorded by Diogenes Laertius 6.54 and Stobaeus, *Eclogae* 3.6.38.

18. φημὶ δεῖν was a turn of phrase used often by Demosthenes.

20. ἂν διαφέροι: B. would make his point better by saying

simply διαφέρει, but he is attempting to display once again his command of the optative.

[διαφέρει is the reading of MS. Auct. T. 4.16, but this can scarcely be anything but emendation by a Renaissance scribe.]

20–2. For the moralists' view about dress cf. Musonius 106.1 and Philo, *De vita contemplativa* 6.55 (Cohn-Wendland). The notion goes back at least as far as Isocrates, *Demonicus* 27.

[21. The MSS. and the Syriac versions are divided between ἱμάτιον and ἱματίων; both seem possible.]

[φέρειν: some MSS. have φορεῖν, which is equally good, but requires ἱματίων for the clausula.]

[ἄν is in DH only, but is essential for the construction unless one assumes that B. made a serious error of syntax.]

22. Notice the elaborate word order, with εἶναι separating the two nouns. ἀλεξητήριον, 'protection', is found at Xenophon, *De re equestri* 5.6.

23ff. φημὶ δεῖν is to be understood as the verb here.

24–5. πλέον ἤ ὡς: πλέον ἤ ὥστε would be expected.

29. ἕξοι: the future optative is the reading of most MSS. instead of the syntactically normal future indicative. In view of B.'s uncertain handling of the optative it may be right here.

30. συνιέντος followed by a genitive of the direct object is a rare construction, cited by LSJ only from *Iliad* 1.273. The precept of 30–1 is found, not in identical words, in Plato, *Alcibiades* I 129e.

[31. δεῖ: δεῖται EYZ, which seems inferior.]

32–3. A reference to the famous maxim γνῶθι σεαυτόν, inscribed on the temple of Apollo at Delphi. It is surprising that B. and other Christians receptive to pagan culture did not notice another Apolline exhortation, ἁμαρτὼν μετανόει, on which see R. Pfeiffer, *Journal of the Warburg and Courtauld Institutes* 25.1952.31–2 (= *Ausgewählte Schriften*, Munich 1960, 69–70).

38. ἐναφιέντων: the only classical authors from whom LSJ cite this word are Herodotus and Aristotle.

39. Most of the ancients believed that certain types of music could have a corrupting influence; here the music

itself is called corrupt. Plato, *Republic* 411a6, uses the phrase
μουσικῇ καταυλεῖν καὶ καταχεῖν τῆς ψυχῆς. For a more sane view
of the matter see the text of Pap. Hibeh 13, perhaps written
by the sophist Hippias.

[καταχεῖν is corrupted to κατασχεῖν by many MSS.]

43–5. Cf. I Kings 16.14–23, 18.10.

45–9. This anecdote about the effect of music in the Dorian
mode on a party of drunken men is told also by Galen, *De
placitis Hippocratis et Platonis* 5.473, but in his version Pythagoras is replaced by the famous fifth-century Athenian
musician Damon. It is at first sight surprising to find B. citing
Pythagoras alongside the book of Kings, but cf. on VII.47–53
and 76 below.

47. σφίσι: αὐτοῖς in classical Attic.

[53. προδήλως DHI and Laud gr. 90: omitted by the other
MSS. and the Syriac versions. The word is unnecessary and
its support in the MS. tradition very slight.]

54. ἀτμούς: 'perfumes', not the classical meaning of the
word.

55. ἑαυτούς: in Hellenistic Greek this reflexive pronoun was
used of the first and second persons as well as the third.

60. τὰ ὑπ' αὐτήν: a similar expression is found at Longus
4.11.2.

συννενευκότας: 'concentrating on'; the nearest analogy seems
to be Clement of Alexandria, *Stromateis* 4.22. The general
notion is found at Plato, *Republic* 586a.

[61 παντὸς MSS. and Syr II: πάντως Boissonade, which is
perhaps right.]

62–4. B. combines a verbatim quotation of Plato, *Republic*
498b6 with a reminiscence of 533d1–2.

65. Cf. Romans 13.14, Galatians 5.13.

67. ἔχοι: one would expect ἔχῃ in a classical writer.

[69. περὶ μὲν τὰ is an attractive variant offered by HX and
Syr II.]

75. The notion of the soul as a charioteer is one of Plato's
most famous ideas (*Phaedrus* 254). The word δυσήνιος seems
to be post-classical.

76–80. This aphorism is attributed to Pythagoras and the

Stoic Crates. It occurs as item 464 in the *Gnomologium Vaticanum*, ed. L. Sternbach.

78. κατασαρκοῦντα is not in LSJ, but Lampe cites several examples from B.

[81. The spelling προϊδόμενον is restored from Vat. gr. 415 and the Tiflis MS.; others have προει–.]

81–2. Was the Academy situated in an unhealthy spot? We may suspect that B. knew this from personal experience, and Aelian, *Varia Historia* 9.10, speaks of it as a νοσηροῦ χωρίου.

83–4. εἰς τὰ περιττά: it is very hard to see why B. did not write here simply περιττήν.

84. φοράν: 'crop'. A severe pruning of the vine can be undertaken in the early summer, and B. means that some of the blossom or berries can be sacrificed. Nevertheless, χλόην, 'foliage' might have been expected.

84–5 is a quotation of Hippocrates, *Aphorisms* 1.3.

86–131 amount to a sermon on wealth, with examples from pagan authors.

86. The word order might more naturally be αὕτη ἡ κτλ.

91. διὰ is unnecessary for the sense.

92–4. The fable of the dragon guarding underground treasure is told by Phaedrus 4.21. I do not know a Greek text of it.

94. ἐπαγρυπνεῖν seems to be a Hellenistic word.

95. δέοι cannot normally have a personal subject: οὐκ ἂν προέλοιτο, πολλοῦ γε δεῖ would be the Attic way of saying this.

97. Λύδιον: i.e. from the river Pactolus. For the expression cf. Clement of Alexandria, *Paidagogos* 3.11.56.4.

98. The gold-bearing ants are from Herodotus 3.102.

103. στάσιμον: 'stable, firm point'.

[105. τοῦ ἴσου: H has τοσούτου, which may be a gloss.]

108. Solon 13.71 (ed. West) (= Theognis 227); it is cited also by Plutarch, *Moralia* 524e.

110–11. Theognis 1155–6. [It is an interesting comment on Byzantine metrical knowledge that nearly all the MSS. ruin the metre of 1155 by an error of word order.]

112. For the story about Diogenes cf. Dio Chrysostom, *Oration* 6.6 (p.85.5 von Arnim). Plutarch, *Moralia* 499b and 604c, cites similar stories.

115. For Pythios see Herodotus 7.27.

117. πλείους ἢ ἀριθμῆσαι: ἢ ὥστε is more usual in this idiom, but see KG 2.503.

[120. εὖ EI and Syr I: other MSS. and Syr II omit; it is not essential and may be a false anticipation of the next line.]

121–3. The anecdote is in Dio Chrysostom, *De regno* 3.1.

122–3. πρὶν ἄν . . . . πειραθῆναι is another departure from standard Attic syntax, as is κεχρῆσθαι meaning no more than χρῆσθαι.

124–8. I have not discovered B.'s source for the comments on Phidias and Polyclitus.

124. ⟨ἐπὶ⟩ τῷ χρυσίῳ μέγα ἐφρόνουν would be more normal Greek.

[125. Instead of Zeus Syr I refers to Ares, which is inexplicable.]

126. The two dual forms are deliberate archaisms, which continued to be affected by Byzantine writers for many centuries.

132. ἀλλὰ δῆτα follows a rejected suggestion; Denniston 10–11, 273.

134. Plato, *Republic* 365c5–6, uses the same two adjectives to describe Archilochus' fox, an animal notorious in ancient literature (cf. frr. 174, 185, 201 West). The rest of this passage has a Platonic tone. At x.2 B. borrows a phrase from the same context, σκιαγραφία ἀρετῆς, but uses it in a different sense.

141. 'The Egyptian sophist' is a curiously allusive way of referring to Proteus. It goes back to Plato, *Euthydemus* 288b8, where Proteus' name is also given. B.'s nephews must have been very sophisticated to catch the allusion.

146. ἥπερ δίκη with the genitive is a usage in late prose, e.g. Arrian, *Anabasis* 3.15.2, 'as is the manner of . . . .'. [This is the reading of H; whether a medieval emendation or not, it seems right. Most MSS. have ὅπερ δίκης, 'which belongs to the manner of . . . .', but I know of no parallel to justify this

construction. MS. Cambridge Dd. 4.16 has ὅπερ δίκην, 'which
is like . . . .'. This appears to be another, less good, emendation.]

147. The behaviour of the polypus had been exploited by
moralists as early as Theognis 215–16.

[149. μεταβαλεῖται H and Syr II, giving a good clausula at
the end of a chapter, is certainly right. Other MSS. mostly
have μεταβάλλεται.]

Chapter X

1. που makes the assertion that we shall learn the same
lessons more completely from the Bible surprisingly diffident.
Did B. really appreciate the nuance of the particle?

2–4. 'For the time being let us give a sketch based on pagan
ideals.' 'Sketch' must be the sense of σκιαγραφία here, and so it
is given in Lampe, but in classical prose the word had the
connotation of 'illusory', being used of trompe l'oeil painting.

3. τό γε νῦν εἶναι: B. alludes again to the youthfulness of his
nephews. εἶναι: cf. v.36.

7–9 are a reference to Hesiod, *Works and Days* 359.

8. καὶ seems pleonastic, but it may have been intended by
B. to strengthen ἡντιναοῦν.

9–14. Bias of Priene (*fl. c.* 560) was another of the Seven
Sages (cf. viii.63). This aphorism is given by Diogenes
Laertius 1.88, but without the accompanying anecdote.

14. Tithonus was proverbial for decrepitude, since Zeus
had granted him eternal life without eternal youth: cf. e.g.
Mimnermus fr. 4 West.

15. Arganthonios, king of Tartessus in Spain, lived to 120,
according to Herodotus 1.163, to 150 according to Lucian,
Macrobioi 10.

16. For Methuselah see Genesis 5.25.

20. ἐπινοίᾳ: 'mind' or 'reflection'. διανοίᾳ might be expected,
had it not already occurred in 19.

23. The proverb is in Leutsch-Schneidewin, *Paroemiographi
graeci* 1.293.

26–31. This is revealed by Plutarch, *Moralia* 602c, to be a Pythagorean precept: ἑλοῦ βίον τὸν ἄριστον, ἡδὺν δὲ αὐτὸν ἡ συνήθεια ποιήσει is his wording of it.

34–6. A rather similar thought is expressed by Plutarch, *Moralia* 81f–82c, which may be B.'s source.

34. τριῶν: if correct this means 'three types'.

τῷ ἀνιάτῳ: προσεοικέναι i.e. 'to resemble the person suffering from the incurable type'. The expression is obscure: one expects an infinitive meaning 'to suffer from'; περιπεπτωκέναι would be standard Attic in this context.

39. εἰς ἀνήκεστον: 'to an incurable state'. μελαγχολίας: 'hopelessness'. The word occurs in the Plutarch passage just cited, but in a different sense.

Appendix: the transmission of the text

In principle the editor of a text in any language, oral literature excepted, attempts to reconstruct or recover the author's
autograph. In the case of many modern and some medieval
authors this autograph still survives intact and makes the
editor's task relatively simple; I say relatively simple because
there are notorious exceptions, such as Dickens' novels, where
the author's alternative versions and changes of mind are
extensive enough to create formidable difficulties of editorial
presentation and decision. No autograph of any ancient
author of note survives, and occasional reports by ancient
critics, who state that they had knowledge of an author's
autograph or of a copy corrected by an author in his own
hand, are by no means above suspicion (J. E. G. Zetzel,
Harvard Studies in classical philology, 77.1973.225–43, especially
230ff.).

For B.'s works we have tantalising scraps of information, or
what purports to be information, about his autographs and
other books that are supposed to have belonged to one of the
charitable institutions he established in Caesarea. The first
of these reports occurs in the chronicle of George Syncellus
(p. 382, lines 7–11, in the Bonn Corpus edition) written about
A.D. 810. He speaks of a book which came into his hands
from the library of Caesarea and bore a note stating that it
had been copied from exemplars collated and corrected by B.
himself. The volume handled by our chronicler did not contain works by B., and he does not give any further evidence
about it that might enable us to quell our suspicion that, even
if it came from Caesarea, its credentials were based on pious
hope rather than factual evidence.

Another tantalising report, perhaps not unconnected with

71

the foregoing, is found in some manuscripts of B.'s ascetic writings. Marginal notes by the scribes in various manuscripts, some of which date from the early years of the tenth century, refer to copies from Pontus, Caesarea and the East; one of the copies in question is stated to have come from the almshouse founded by B. in Caesarea. The notes are doubtless earlier than any of the manuscripts which carry them, and J. Gribomont has ingeniously pointed out that one of them, when compared with the Syriac translation of B., proves that the notes should be dated to the sixth century at the latest (*Histoire du texte des Ascétiques de S. Basile*, Louvain 1953, 151–64, 325–6). So there is evidence for editorial activity on the text of B. at this early date. Unfortunately we cannot say how it affected the text of B.'s other works, including the present essay.

The earliest witnesses to the text are two translations into Syriac, neither of which has been taken into account by previous editors. Their existence is revealed by A. Baumstark's *Geschichte der syrischen Literatur*, Bonn 1922, 78, 261 and cf. 248. The earlier is found in two sixth-century manuscripts in the British Museum (Add. 14543 = Syriac 550 and Add. 17144 = Syriac 732), and the translation itself is thought to have been made in the fifth century. The other is in a ninth-century manuscript in the Cambridge University Library (Add. 3175), and was most probably made in the seventh century. It does not of course follow that an editor ought to abandon the Greek manuscripts in favour of these earlier witnesses, since there is never any guarantee that an old manuscript will have a better text than a later one, or that the Oriental translators were equal to the difficulties that confronted them. However, I have thought it worth while to consult the versions at a few points where the Greek manuscripts disagree or offer a dubious text, to see if it is possible to determine what reading they imply. Although this has occasionally been helpful, the fact remains that the Syriac translators sometimes did no more than paraphrase the text and at certain points they were clearly unable to grasp its meaning.

Appendix: the transmission of the text

From the end of the ninth century onwards the text was copied very frequently in Byzantium. The oldest manuscript carrying an exact date is in the Hunterian Museum in Glasgow, MS. 407–8, which was signed and dated by the scribe Ignatios in the year 899. I have collated this book and recorded the few results worthy of note in the commentary. Apart from its age the book has been thought to have a certain importance from the fact that it is said to be a product of the Stoudios monastery in Constantinople (R. Devreesse, *Introduction à l'étude des manuscrits grecs*, Paris 1954, 32). This fact if true would be of some potential significance, since that monastery was the home of St. Theodore (d. 813) who prepared a new edition of the ascetic writings of B. and may have had excellent copies of all his works. The ascription, however, seems to be without foundation; no evidence was adduced in support of it and I have not been able to find any.

Another old manuscript which I thought it worth while to collate is Vaticanus gr. 415, from the early years of the tenth century. This too has been ascribed to the Stoudios monastery, for no other reason than that the first page of each quire is marked with two or more crosses at the top (C. Giannelli, *Studi bizantini e neoellenici* 10.1963.225 n.3). This ground is quite inadequate, since there are manuscripts from other centres with the same markings (N. G. Wilson, *Medieval Greek bookhands*, Cambridge, Mass. 1973, 18).

The transmission of a text as widely read as B. is so comlicated that there is no hope of classifying the manuscripts exactly by what are called stemmatic principles. In such a situation editors often try to establish groupings of manuscripts which show a general affinity to each other. This method has been applied recently by S. Y. Rudberg in his edition *L'homélie de Basile de Césarée sur le mot 'Observe toi-même'*, Stockholm 1962. He collated the manuscripts and divided them into fourteen classes. It would be useful if the same classes were found to be valid for other homilies, but this unfortunately is not so. For instance, the two manuscripts of the present essay which coincide most markedly in their readings as cited by Boulenger are his G and H (Paris. gr. 497 and 498), which would on his

73

evidence belong to the same group and perhaps form a group of their own. But on the evidence assembled by Rudberg for the edition of the other homily they belong to the groups which he designates by the numbers 5 and 11. Another test of the same kind led to an equally negative result: collating the Oxford manuscript Laud gr. 90 I found that its closest affinity seemed to be with MS. E (Paris. gr. 487) and that it also had some relation to G and H. According to Rudberg the Laud MS. belongs to group 12, whereas E is in group 3. For the editor who believes that further collation is subject to the law of diminishing returns there seems to be no satisfactory method of making progress. I did however collate a few late manuscripts to form an impression of the extent of Renaissance emendation, and also looked at the manuscript discovered by K. Treu in Tiflis, which was brought to my attention by Rudberg (*op. cit.* 120–5); he thought that it may have been written in southern Italy or Sicily, and that it could indicate the existence of a somewhat divergent text current in one of the provinces of the Byzantine world. According to Rudberg it belonged to his group 4, and since Boulenger appeared not to have collated any book ascribed by Rudberg to this group, I examined it, but with very little gain.

Since there are innumerable manuscripts, of which no stemma can be constructed, it is difficult to make a suitable list of witnesses to be cited. A very long apparatus criticus is beyond the scope of this edition and would inevitably contain a great deal of dross. As a practical compromise, which has the merit of convenience and brevity, I have decided to cite most of the early manuscripts known to Boulenger, adding a number of readings from those that I have collated myself where their variants seemed interesting. As a rule it is possible to dispense with the later manuscripts listed by Boulenger. I think that my notes deal with every variant of any significance as well as a number of quite minor details.

The MSS. cited from Boulenger are:

Paris. gr. 476   A   10th c.
  do.   480   B   10th c.

do.	481	C	11th c.
do.	482	D	11th c.
do.	487	E	11th c.
do.	498	H	10th c.
do.	500	I	11th c.
Paris. Coislin	47	Y	11th c.
do.	48	X	11th c.
do.	50	Z	11th c.

Except in the case of H, which I have inspected myself and dated a century earlier than Boulenger, the dates given are those assigned by him. I eliminated his G (Paris. gr. 497) because on inspection it turned out to be no earlier than H and it offers no interesting distinctive readings. His F and V did not seem to offer enough to justify mention.

The MSS. that I have collated myself are:

Cambridge, University Library Dd. 4.16	15th c.
Glasgow, Hunterian Museum 407–8	A.D. 899
Oxford, Laud gr. 90	13th or 14th c.
ibid., Auct. T. 4.16	15th c.
Rome, Vaticanus gr. 415	10th c.
Tiflis, Academy of Sciences, unnumbered MS.	10th c.